1

Practising Jesus

Chris Beales

Rainmaker Books 2013

First published in 2013 by
Rainmaker Books
30 Church Road, Woburn Sands,
Milton Keynes MK17 8TA

A catalogue of this book is available
from the British Library

ISBN 978-1-909863-00-2

Typeset by Maybe Magazine,
Acorn House, 381, Midsummer Boulevard,
Milton Keynes MK9 3HP

Printed and bound by Micropress

Acknowledgements

This work is a product of the ideas and actions of all kinds of people who have inspired and influenced me over many years. My wife Angela and children Jackie, Chris and Andrew and their families are a constant source of inspiration and challenge, reminding me always of the need to earth my dreams in reality. I am grateful to them for their love and patience. I am grateful too to a number of friends who have looked thoughtfully and critically at early drafts of this book and commented – among them Evelyn Wright, Ralph Willcox, Dave Burns, Peter Sedgwick, John Atherton, Shola Lana, Wilf Wilde, Peter Challen and Paul Skirrow. Phil Green and Callum McHugh kindly helped with getting the manuscript typeset and printed. The money raised from sales of this book will go towards the funding of a Community Worker in Woburn Sands and our ministry in Woburn Sands.

Thank you

Chris Beales
Woburn Sands
May 2014

FOREWORD

Don't read this book unless you are willing to be challenged and unsettled about your faith and the way that it is possible for Christians to make an impact on society today.

Chris Beales has had a life-long passion to make a real difference to the lives of ordinary people both here in the UK and abroad. This book tells of the way his faith has changed and developed over the years since he was first ordained in 1976 and began ministering in Leeds. Since then he has lived in various part of the United Kingdom, and worked for the Church of England, charities and the government.

Determined to bridge the gap between the sacred and the secular, nothing has ever been off-limits as Chris has collaborated with people of different faiths or of no faith, both through co-operatives as well as other groups such as Slipstream, the National Gospel Development Agency and Afghan Action, which trains carpet weavers in Kabul and sells their products here in the UK. Aware of the lack of skilled workers in the UK, Chris Beales has also been involved in the development of University Technical Colleges, an exciting new initiative where teenagers are trained in vocational skills.

Chris concludes his book by reflecting on his life and experience in the light of St Paul, who was also an entrepreneur. I hope this book will stimulate and challenge many people to apply their faith in practical ways in the world today.

Dr Alan Smith
Bishop of St Albans
25 April 2013

INTRODUCTION: WHAT THE BOOK IS FOR

I'm one of those people who'd like to write great stories. But they never quite get beyond my head and down on paper. There are always lots of good reasons why not. So the opportunity to take some time out on sabbatical, kindly offered by the Diocese of St Albans, has given me the chance to do several things I'm not very good at.

First, to rest, relax, think and pray.

Secondly, to do some research into something I have long been concerned about, youth unemployment. I refer to this in more detail in Chapter 8, below.

And thirdly, to do some reading of current theological thinking about St Paul. I have always done lots of reading, though not in a very disciplined way. So this time, I've taken the opportunity to consult an expert – Professor of Theology John Barclay, in my old University of Durham – and I have hungrily devoured some fascinating material. My final chapter describes what I have been discovering.

The fourth thing is to get down to doing some writing. I have always wanted to be a writer and now's my chance. I have been drafting material for a book for over 20 years and, one day, perhaps it will emerge into the light. In the meantime, I have several things I want to write – so here goes.

The title for this book is *Practising Jesus*. I have been 'practising Jesus' – trying to live the life of Christ - for nearly half a century and, the older I get, the more I realise I have so much to learn and the more I recognise my shortcomings and inadequacies.

I was very impressed with a book I read last year by Matthew Syed, British journalist, broadcaster and author of *Bounce*, described as "a must-read for anyone interested in the science of success, and the mindset and culture that support it". His basic premise is an encouragement for us all. There are not a minority of brilliant people, each born a genius and supremely better than us mere mortals – but there are some brilliant people around who have taken their degree of natural talent and hugely enhanced it by practise, practise, practise.

I suppose the challenges that have driven me are these: how to make sense of God and Christian faith in today's world and how to live out the gospel in the midst of all the pressures and compromises of daily life. *'Practising Jesus'* is not easy. But Jesus never said it would be.

CHAPTER 1
ST MICHAEL'S CHURCH, WOBURN SANDS

In September 2008 I became the priest in charge of St Michael Woburn Sands, my first parish in over 30 years of ordained ministry. The arrangement was that I should serve 2 days a week, on a Sunday and a weekday, for which we would be provided with a house, the vicarage. After a year, the work had grown and I became half time stipendiary. In December 2011, a letter from the Diocesan Office to the Secretary of the PCC said that the Church was now no longer a 'suspended benefice' (as it had been for 5 years following problems in 2006) and I could be appointed Vicar under 'common tenure'.

Being at St Michael's has been quite a surprise for me. For the best part of four decades, I had been involved in all kinds of things other than parish ministry and have always hung a bit loose to the institution - my theological college tutor, Ian Bunting, used to say that he thought I would always be hovering somewhere on the margin between Church and world. When I was at theological college, I went through a lot of soul searching and wondered whether I really was cut out for ordained ministry. Ian stuck by me and, I felt, really believed in me when I didn't really believe in myself. So the parochial ministry for which I was trained in the early 1970s took a long time to reach its fulfilment!

I worked for the Church of England's General Synod at Church House, Westminster from 1985 – 91 and used sometimes, somewhat cheekily, to describe the work of bishops in the Church of England as mainly being about "the management of graceful decline". The former Bishop of Hereford, John Oliver, once commented "there's nothing graceful about it".

I have often wondered whether the reasons for decline are not unrelated to the ponderous structures of the Church of England, with its regulations and bureaucracy and committees and, too often, lack of transparency. Or maybe its message has just not caught up with where people are at nowadays. I have reflected on the possible link between decline and the grouping together of parishes under the pastoral care of one harassed, overworked cleric. I have considered the arguments of secularism, which certainly contain much truth but do not tell the whole story. I have noticed the powerful, not very subtle forces of scarcity of time, pressure of work and consumerism and their effect on us all. I have seen the impact on Sundays – and, therefore, on Church attendance and corporate worship - of Sunday trading and Sunday sport. And I have wondered why we insist on mainly measuring the presence and actions of God by Sunday attendance at Church, when a multiplicity of other important factors should be considered.

It is not all doom and gloom. So here's a question: what is it that seems to be making our own parish Church, and many others, grow? Of course, divine grace is rather important! And growth in numbers isn't the whole story – there are many faithful congregations which appear small and isolated but which are deeply rooted in real faith and commitment, making a sustained and powerful impact in their communities. But why are we at St Michael's apparently growing rather than shrinking in attendance and impact?

Woburn Sands is a great place to live and the community is active and engaging. The congregation has more than doubled in the past four years. I have wonderful colleagues and we have been encouraged by the involvement of a number of young families. Our children's work is thriving and we are looking to appoint a community worker with a particular focus on the new housing area, Parklands, at the far end of the village – which now accounts for more than a quarter of the village population.

In December 2008, we used a series of six Advent Group meetings to work together on our Vision for St Michael's, and this has been helpful to us as we have sought to implement it and make a real difference in and contribution to the wider community – both local and international.

Our vision for St Michael's is

• To be people of prayer and action, loving and trusting God and serving others…
• To be a place where all can belong, are welcomed and accepted and feel supported and inspired…
• To be peacemakers, with all others of good will, in the struggle for a just and peaceful world.

Our links with the two other local Churches, Catholic and Methodist, are growing steadily stronger and, under the auspices of Churches Together in Woburn Sands, we try to make our community engagement as ecumenical as possible. Good examples of joint work are *Christian News*, our Church magazine, youth work in the community, provision of a shelter for homeless people through the winter, support for the Milton Keynes Food Bank and support for several international projects - and, of course, our Parklands project.

Why are we at St Michael's apparently growing rather than shrinking in attendance and impact? Here are a few stabs at a hesitant response to what may not even be the right question!

First, we are our own parish. We are not combined with any others – we were for a short time some years ago, with disastrous results. We have our own parish priest, albeit not full time, and we have a huge amount of 'ministry' being exercised by fellow unpaid clergy and our lay reader as well as many members of the congregation. If nothing else, I know I have done one good thing since coming to St Michael's in September 2008: I've encouraged people to carry on doing what they can to serve God and others.

In my early days, people used to check with me: "Is it alright if I…?". My answer, almost invariably, has been Yes with a capital Y. I firmly believe that the Church's 'ministry' involves us all and each has a part to play. Of course, there are some things only I and my fellow clergy, Nick Parkinson and Ralph Willcox, can do, like celebrate the Eucharist or conduct marriages. But there are lots of other things which need doing if our Church is to 'practise Jesus' in the community.

Being a parish on our own is not intended to mean that we are an independent fiefdom. But having a sense of identity and belonging is important, never more so than when the community we serve starts to grow rapidly – as is happening to Woburn Sands.

Secondly, speaking personally, I am only the half time parish priest. This gives me considerable freedom to choose where to invest time and energy – and where not to. I sometimes regret not being able to offer more to the wider Church, but, on the other hand, I feel under no obligation to join committees or attend meetings where my presence is not going to make much difference to anyone or anything.

I am quite surprised at the amount of administration clergy have to manage. It is not so onerous as to be all-consuming, but there is enough of it to make me think that a parish administrator would actually be rather helpful. In our parish, we currently have other priorities so this will have to wait.

I am happy to try and offer leadership without having to micro-manage people. The joy of working with volunteers is that they are, by definition, making a commitment to carry out what they offer. But, as someone has remarked, managing volunteers can be like herding cats! Our volunteers at St Michael's tend to be people who are self starters and much of what they do is quiet, hidden and personal. One issue we face is finding new people to take on the work our current volunteers have developed over a number of years. This doesn't happen easily. I suppose that, in practise, some things reach crisis point, or even die, before new things, with new instigators, appear. The Church is constantly having to reinvent its activity and service.

One of the benefits of not being full time is not becoming too anxious when people, especially some of our newer members, are not in Church every Sunday. Busy and complex lives and family demands mean that some people are regular attenders on Sundays – but regular may mean every three or four weeks.

Sundays are not the only time when people live out their faith – thank goodness. So letting people get on with God and things should be entirely appropriate. In fact, the life of a Church is best demonstrated in the service which goes on throughout the week. We have few formal activities on weekdays. And when we hold things like Advent and Lent Groups, they are not very well attended - I'm not really sure why.

Thirdly, our Sunday services, though traditional in many ways, do seem to scratch where many people are itching. We try to be fairly light and informal, though within a structure which can be easily followed by visitors. We encourage participation and are increasingly involving different people in leading worship. We also try to cultivate a strong sense of belonging, with coffee time after the service being particularly important. Most people really appreciate the friendliness, but we have had the odd comment from people who have felt ignored while others were meeting and greeting each other. The clergy usually stand at the door and are able to catch up with those leaving. Of course, conversations don't go very deep at the door, but occasionally important information is supplied, which can then be followed up.

This is all very basic stuff and thousands of Churches do exactly the same.

Fourthly, we take ecumenism seriously. We are not ecumaniacs but we are, gradually, becoming closer to our Catholic and Methodist friends and sharing both in worship and service. Churches Together has become a mechanism for doing things with one another in the Churches and also with the wider community. In fact, we have reached a kind of agreement that we should share our 'outward facing' activities as far as possible. That is beginning to make an impact on our work together, especially in relation to support for homeless people through the winter, or our youth activities, or our international connections.

The idea of recruiting a young, dynamic community worker has been buzzing around for a while. With the influx of newcomers, mainly in the Parklands Estate, we have been considering how best to respond. Over the past three years, we have delivered invitations to events around the houses and held local activities at Christmas time. In May 2012, we set about raising the funding needed to recruit and appoint a community worker – whose brief is mainly about being around the place and getting to know people, sussing out what the issues challenging the local residents are and how they might be addressed - and trying to discover whether there are opportunities for developing any projects or programmes there. Although St Michael's has, initially, acted as the lead partner, this is very much a joint initiative involving the Catholic and Methodist Churches.

Fifthly, we have a lively group of children and young people, up to about 14 years old. They are well led and enjoy their activities. The congregation enjoy having them and I hear very few complaints about any noise they may make or distraction they may cause. We have not yet resolved the question of admitting children to Communion and we could be doing far more to provide support for young believers, especially recently confirmed youngsters.

Needless to say, we have many weaknesses in addition to those referred to above. Our age and ethnic profile probably reflects the wider community, apart from the gap we have in young adults aged between 14 and 25. But I sense that we could be doing more to help people go deeper on their journey of faith. Woburn Sands is by no means a poor community and it is not ethnically diverse, though becoming more so with the influx of new residents in Parklands. It does have a lot of older people, with five care homes or sheltered living facilities as well as many older people living at home. An important part of the Church's service in the community relates to visiting and supporting the elderly and we have recognised the need to reflect on this and extend what we do in more strategic and effective ways.

Last year, we installed a new heating system in the Church and began to explore with the congregation what other improvements to the building we might undertake to make it more fit for purpose. As part of that process, we asked these questions:

• How best can we use the wonderful resources of our building and churchyard to love and serve God and our neighbours?
• What should we be thinking of doing to make the Church 'fit for the future' – for at least the next 50 years of its life and service here?

Of course, it could be pretty much the same as now – though increasing costs and the ravages of time may make that hard to achieve. In terms of location, we are up a hill and, at the moment, have no adequate parking. We are out of the main part of the village and therefore unable to benefit much from 'passing trade'. And our building needs to become more adaptable, so that it can be used for other purposes (such as concerts, plays and performances) and for smaller groups needing meeting space, if it is to be sustainable.

Given the national need for more housing, I wonder whether, over the next half a century, Churches like St Michael's – especially those in rural areas where congregations are small and costs increasingly unsustainable - will be adapted to provide homes for local people. Or, as already happens in some places, into shops, post offices, creches and nurseries, day care centres and much more. With worship space included in the complex.

All this seems a very long way from the New Testament notion of Church, or 'ecclesia'. In Chapter 12, I take a closer look at the Apostle

Paul, particularly trying to see where his thinking and ideas might impinge on the life and experience of the Church in today's complex and dangerous world, a world shaped and dominated by competing economic and social forces over which we have so little influence.

In Chapters 10 and 11, I come back to St Michael's with a selection of six *Christian News* articles and some sermons (from present and past situations). Meanwhile, Chapters 2 to 9 attempt to trace my own journey and theological development. If that seems a bit self indulgent, what I really hope is that, by telling the story of my journey, there will be points of contact or connection which others can make with their own journeys through life and their own ways of discovering God and practising Jesus.

CHAPTER 2

EARLY FORMATION

I have always sensed that God's vision for humanity and the world should be bigger than just the salvation of individual souls. My faith became real for me at a Scripture Union camp in 1966 and over the next few years I was nurtured in the Scriptures, learning to read and apply them in my own life of faith and discipleship. I am deeply grateful for this grounding in biblical faith and understanding. It didn't take long for me to realise that personal faith in Jesus Christ was not the end of the story, but just the beginning!

I was lucky enough in 1967 to meet my great cricketing hero, David Sheppard, then working at the Mayflower Centre in Canning Town, East London (later to become the Bishop of Liverpool). He invited me to visit the Mayflower Centre that summer and I still recall being taken to the roof of the Centre to look down on a group of boys playing football. "He's a natural leader.." said David, pointing to one boy, "he's a bright kid..", pointing to another, "but most of them will be in trouble with the law and even end up inside..".

I was invited to spend a week staying at an inner city vicarage in South London – Kennington Oval, to be precise, the home of Surrey County Cricket Club and the location of a large and imposing church, St Mark's, right opposite the Oval tube station. The vicar, Colin Scott, was just serving lunch when the doorbell rang.

"'Allo Mr Scotty dog" came a teenage voice. And I was soon knocking around the streets of Kennington with a gang of lads who lived in the blocks of flats around the cricket ground, all of which are named after 19th century Surrey cricketers. It was an eye opener for me and I got to know this group and the area over several years of returning to the Oval for children's summer holiday bible clubs and youth club camps. On one camp, in Chigwell, Essex, it rained so much that all our tents were swamped and even the underground line was flooded. A week later, one of the teenage girls in the group was blinded by airgun pellets from a gun which one of the boys had fired at her – but she wouldn't tell the police who it was and no one was ever convicted.

When I went as an undergraduate to Durham University, I quickly became involved with a Council estate on the edge of the City, notorious as a dumping ground but full of all kinds of people, good hearted and hard working as well as rogues and folk down on their luck.

It was a formative and disturbing period. Some years later, married and with two small children, I was a half time industrial chaplain and half time curate in West Leeds, working in a daughter church serving two Council estates and some streets of old back-to-backs. I was reading all sorts of radical writers at the time, the most influential of whom was Paulo Friere. I warmed to the Brazilian philosopher Friere's ideas of 'conscientisation' – in which people should be the 'subjects' of their own destiny, not the 'objects' of other people's decisions. I devised a confirmation course for young people in the local estates which attempted to draw on his thinking. Without, I'm afraid, a great deal of success!

What follows is a bit of a mix. I have included a selection of talks and articles from the past 30 years, concluding with a selection of *Christian News* articles I've written and a few (a very few!) sermons. My final chapter reflects what I have been reading and learning about St Paul.

The first article was penned to set out my commitment to that bigger vision I had been moving towards during my student years. I wrote this in 1979, during my time as a curate and industrial chaplain in Leeds. I think I'd probably write something pretty similar today.

ARTICLE FOR THE PARISH MAGAZINE OF CHRIST CHURCH UPPER ARMLEY January 1979.

In a discussion amongst clergy about our aims and objectives, one minister said that, as pastor and leader of a thriving town centre Church with a large gathered congregation, his aim was "to build a praising people" – and having done that, the Church would then be in a position to minister powerfully in the neighbourhood.

Whilst acknowledging the many good fruits of this Church's life and vigour, it has to be said that, for several years now, this building process has been going on but it is still no nearer its goal. In fact I would suggest that such a goal will never be achieved.. and any deliberate movement in that direction can only have severely negative repercussions for the Church in its calling to serve God in the world.

The goal is unashamedly inward looking. In practise, it emphasises the life of the Church to the virtual exclusion of life in society at large. And it reduces the Kingdom of God to some ecclesiastical sanctuary for saints. Of course, outsiders are welcomed into the fold, where they are helped to draw near to God – as he is experienced in the gathering of the faithful – but emotionally and in other more concrete ways they are gradually withdrawn from the hazards of secular society. The clear, if unstated, intention is to ensure individuals a place in heaven rather than hell, and in the meantime to provide a loving Church fellowship, which, in becoming a 'praising people', starts to act like a magnet, drawing people to the Lord by 'being him' in praise and worship.

Salvation, then, is understood individually – a person must respond to God's call by commitment to him; and corporately – membership and active involvement in the life of the local Church are essential.

Many Churches are growing strong with such a goal at the (conscious or unconscious) heart of their ministry. But the theology underlying such practise is often rather weak. What really seems to count is the heart-felt and genuine desire to be 'alive'. Such a desire, expressed in prayer and service, leads to a genuine sense of community, which, besides being attractive, also offers security, acceptance, and the chance to be useful in giving of one's talents and abilities. And to the extent that it produces commitment to and love for other people, it can be said that the Holy Spirit is at work.

But without any clear theological framework as a basis, the work of the Holy Spirit must inevitably be restricted. A desire to be alive may not be enough, because all too often the methods adopted to achieve this end are exclusive and inward-looking, as I have already said. Although there might be a strong emphasis on fellowship, community, love, commitment and service in the Body of Christ, such an emphasis is incomplete if it is not tempered with the judgment of God. It is through God's words and acts of judgment that true love is discovered and practised. For example, God's judgment will go against us if we neglect the poor and the needy, the hungry and the thirsty, the prisoners, the oppressed, the widows and the orphans. In fact, according to Jesus, Judgment Day will come as a nasty shock for us if we ignore the costly demands of discipleship and love for others. The parable of the sheep and goats (Matthew 25) spells this out clearly – Jesus identifies himself personally with the hungry, thirsty, foreign, sick and imprisoned. "I tell you this, whenever you did this for one of the least important of these brothers of mine, you did it for me". Without a starting point that looks beyond the Church for the activity of God, we restrict the Holy Spirit in his activity in the world.

We begin, then, with the assertion that God is the creator of the world, and is at work in the world even where the Church may not be recognisably present. If God is only active among the redeemed who gather together in Church – if we equate the Church with God's Kingdom – then how can we explain the enormous credibility gap between an All-Mighty God and a world which seems to carry on perfectly happily (?) without having to name him? In other words, do we honestly believe that God's work is restricted to the fallible, naïve, divided and muddled Body that claims to be his People? Moreover, our reading of the Bible prevents us from assuming that God does not use for his purposes people outside the Chosen People ("Cyrus my servant", for example, in Isaiah).

If we start theologically with the 'world' rather than the 'Church' to discover what God is getting up to, our next step will be to look around carefully for any signs or indications of God's activity in our midst, in the everyday events of life. Bear in mind the parable of the sheep and the goats – and we would be justified in thinking that God's activity is as much to be seen in the loving acts of self-sacrifice of some caring person down the street (regardless of whether they ever darkened the Church's doors) as in the enthusiastic reports of a prayer and praise meeting at which "God was really present".

Now we can make theological sense of the many things going on around us which are motivated by love (at least in part.. our motives are never always entirely what they might be!). We can see God at work in many exciting ways – acts of costly love towards a neighbour, people concerned for the poor of the Third World, people standing against racism, groups attempting to create a climate of freedom and responsibility in the face of some heartless bureaucracy, and so on.

Accepting that God is at work in his world and spotting some signs of the Kingdom makes us ask what we should learn from all this. No longer can we presume to have the Good News neatly packaged and ready to impart to the hungry masses (if they'd only listen). Instead we begin to see that it must be understood and applied only through open, genuine and reciprocal encounter with other human beings and the world. Thus we arrive at Mission – and our part in God's great mission in and to his world.

There are two routes to Mission based on the theological starting points identified:

• Church-centred theology: build up the congregation; develop into a magnetic community attracting people into the Body through praise and worship; move out into the world in service;
• World-centred theology: identify where God is at work in the world; get involved in and with those signs of the Kingdom (breaking down barriers between Church members and others); give and receive Good News in this context, by latching onto people and situations where they're at; and move on to develop

caring and open communities. The Church in this model is an aid to Mission, not the end.

I have attempted to show briefly the inadequacy of a theology which does not go much beyond wanting to serve God successfully by being a live Church. I have been critical of a theology which limits God's activity to the Church and individual salvation. I am convinced that Church-centred theology can never hope to make any significant or lasting impact in British society. Without a theology which actually sees God already at work outside the Church, we either put our heads in the sand (as many of us do) or give up in despair. God's mission has to do with the redemption of his world – and if we settle for less, we are untrue to his high calling.

THE KINGDOM OF GOD – MEANING AND PURPOSE

Some months after drafting my article about Church- and world-centred theology, the Leeds Industrial Mission, with whom I worked, organised a debate on mission and evangelism, with two well known speakers from very different theological positions – David Watson, probably the best known evangelist in the country, based in York and travelling the world to speak at students' gatherings and Church missions, and David Jenkins, newly arrived in Leeds as Professor of Theology and later to become Bishop of Durham and an outspoken critic of Prime Minister Margaret Thatcher. It was interesting and encouraging that both the 'evangelical', David Watson and the 'liberal', David Jenkins, agreed on far more than they disagreed about. Their understanding of God's Kingdom and its outworking was cosmic as well as personal. They described their experience of God's Spirit at work in the world and in communities in similar terms.

I was part of another group at this time, convened by one of David Jenkins' academic colleagues in the Leeds Theology Department, Haddon Willmer, which brought together representatives of Industrial Mission thinking and practise with representatives of evangelical theology and practise. John Gladwin and Graham Dow – both were to become Anglican diocesan bishops – were involved on the evangelical side, and, from Industrial Mission, John Atherton (one of the most articulate writers on theology and economics in the past three decades), Geoffrey Sturman (who founded the Hull University Theology in an Industrial Society post graduate course and trained many industrial missioners in the '70s and '80s) and Ray Taylor (a dynamic Baptist working in Newport, South Wales with the steel industry and the thousands of unemployed steel workers and miners in the Valleys). Margaret Kane was also part of the group. She was a professional theologian who had worked with the Sheffield Industrial Mission in the 1960s before going to set up IM in Hong Kong and then returning to the UK to become the Bishop of Durham's theological consultant on industrial and economic matters in the north east of England. She was, some years later, to become a great spiritual and theological resource to me when we moved to Teesside.

I felt a bit of a pipsqueak among giants at this gathering – but it is interesting to note, again, the convergence in IM and evangelical thinking. Maybe the evangelical input was untypical. But it resonates with the most socially aware and significant evangelical theology in the country today, which has become deeply embedded in social issues, takes injustice and ecology seriously, recognises the importance of engaging in cross-faith dialogue and relationships and sits somewhat uneasily with the 'fortress Christianity' positions of those who feel they must defend their version of the faith against all alternative perspectives – especially to do with sexuality or women bishops.

A significant event several months earlier had been my attendance, in November 1978, at a big evangelistic rally in Leeds Town Hall. A well known American evangelist, Nicky Cruz, was billed to speak and I got together a busload of local people, including our Church's cub leader and the convenor of shop stewards at the works I visited as an industrial chaplain. Nicky Cruz arrived 40 minutes late, after an excruciating musical interlude led by the Don Summers Crusade and a doctor from a local – highly charismatic – Baptist Church, part of what a friend rudely called the 'Jesus up your jumper' brigade.

Nicky Cruz, made famous in a book written in the late '50s about New York gang warfare, *The Cross and the Switchblade*, didn't have a lot to say, though he said it at great length. It mainly consisted of how much Jesus loved him and – with impressive crocodile tears at his sinfulness all those years ago – how much the pastor, Davey, loved him. When the appeal came and the electric organ began to play, teenagers flocked forward and I felt distinctly uncomfortable. Then there was an appeal for more counsellors – and who knows what kind of volunteers went forward to assist at that point? I became distinctly cross.

I wrote soon afterwards to the organiser, a local, well intentioned vicar of one of the prominent evangelical Churches in the city, to voice my dis-ease.

He called a meeting of ministers, which I attended, though with a temperature of over 100 I was in no fit state to argue my cause. He dismissed the criticism by quoting someone who told him "While Nicky spoke, everything just fell into place..". The local hospital chaplain then went on to tell us about a shop steward representing striking health workers – it was during the Winter of Discontent (1978/79) – who was now on his deathbed with cancer. The chaplain told us how he had spoken directly to this man. "Your past is meaningless", he had said, "the only thing that matters is your eternal future.."

At this point, my temperature rose another 10 degrees and I exploded – mainly due to my pent up frustration with the discussion so far.

"So what you're saying", I blustered, "is that nothing we do has any significance except in relation to our ultimate spiritual state.. This man had given his life to supporting low paid and undervalued health service workers. Surely that has some meaning, some worth to God?"

For what it's worth, I think that I would date this point in my life as the point at which I ceased to be an evangelical – though that is not the same as losing my passion for God and the gospel. In fact, I refuse to be labelled and believe that the dreary debates which so occupy many clergy have little to do with 'Good News' – they're more like 'bad olds', and are unrelated to the things which really determine the future of the world.

The importance to my own spiritual journey of seeing God at work in the world and outside the Church cannot be overstated. But it does beg an underlying question: what is the Church actually for? And, if a Church is not being what it should be – reflective of the life and love of Christ and thoroughly engaged in society – does it therefore invalidate its very being? Does it cease to be 'Church'?

It is not, of course, for us to judge. But we should perhaps be mindful at all times that the Church is a human institution and, as such, subject to the limitations and foibles of humankind as much as any other institution. It can also be argued that Jesus almost certainly didn't envisage what, over twenty centuries, we have become.

CHAPTER 3

GOD AND ECONOMY

From Leeds we moved to Hartlepool, a steel and shipbuilding town on the north east coast which, by the early 1980s, was suffering severely from deindustrialisation with the collapse of British manufacturing. I was a full time industrial chaplain with the Teesside Industrial Mission (TIM) and witnessed the death of industry in the town. I worked with companies large and small, including British Steel, GEC and Ever Ready. Despite the problems, it was a time of huge opportunity and I became involved in training and job creation projects which gave me invaluable experience, even though, in the case of the Hartlepool Co-operative Enterprise Centre, we had to go into liquidation after a year.

HARTLEPOOL CO-OPERATIVE ENTERPRISE CENTRE

My vision for co-operatives had started at a War on Want meeting. I began to read around the subject and invited to one of the TIM team meetings the local branch manager of the Co-op Bank – who began by saying that no one had ever asked him about co-operatives before, but he'd go away and find out about them! Later that year, a documentary programme on BBC2, *Horizon*, reported on the development of co-operatives which had originated in the mid-1950s with a priest and some apprentices in the Basque town of Mondragon and had, by 1980, 18,000 members and a whole range of co-operative companies and organisations, including schools and colleges, hospitals and manufacturing and service industries. 35 years later, the Mondragon Corporation has grown extensively and spread across the world, as described by Race Matthews, a former Australian Government Minister and long time supporter of the Mondragon model..

> The essentials of the Mondragon story are simple. What arose in 1956 as a handful of workers in a disused factory, using hand tools and sheet metal to make oil-fired heating and

cooking stoves is today a massive conglomerate of some 260 manufacturing, retail, financial, agricultural, civil engineering and support co-operatives and associated entities, with jobs for 83,800 workers, and annual sales in excess of $US20 billion.

Mondragon co-operatives now own or joint venture some 114 local and overseas subsidiaries, and are committed to their conversion to employee ownership on a case-by-case basis, consistent with local laws, customs and other cultural and economic considerations.

As equal co-owners of their workplaces, members enjoy job security together with individual capital holdings, equal sharing of profits on a proportionate basis and an equal 'one-member one vote' say in their governance. Remuneration within the cooperatives is egalitarian, with the highest rates payable other than in exceptional circumstances being no greater than six and a half times the lowest.

And members share at one remove in ownership of a unique system of secondary support co-operatives, from which the primary or frontline co-operatives draw resources including financial services, social insurance, education and training and research and development.

Back in 1980, I was so excited by the Mondragon story that I hired the *Horizon* video from the BBC and showed it all over Teesside, including to the full Hartlepool Council. Soon after, Cleveland County Council set up the Cleveland Co-operative Agency and I became a member of the Board. In Hartlepool, the Anglican Churches in the Deanery agreed to raise £5000 and that set the ball rolling for what became the Hartlepool Co-operative Enterprise Centre. We raised another £300,000 from local authority, Government, European and other sources and the Archbishop of York conducted a grand opening in June 1982 in our factory premises on an industrial estate in the town.

Our aim was to provide 50 unemployed young people aged between

18 and 25 with skills training and a chance to own and run their own co-operative business in a sheltered environment with lots of business support. For a while, things flourished. One co-op, doing bicycle repairs and selling reconditioned bikes, was featured in *The Sunday Times*. Run by 18 year old twin brothers, the Kinnersleys, it was building up nicely until someone broke into the premises and stole the bikes. Sadly, that dashed their hopes. Another co-op, with two ex-employees from a Japanese company based in Peterlee and two young trainees, focused on recalibrating industrial measuring instruments. Again, it was going so well – until one of the members started having marital problems and was knocked off course.

In the August of that year, I was on holiday, as was the Company Chairman, the Anglican Rural Dean, David Ogden when, in our absence, the decision was taken to close several of the co-ops and use the labour to focus on making sunbeds. Wood and lamps were purchased and sales were guaranteed – until the company we were supplying disappeared without notice, leaving us with £15,000 of stock and owing £10,000 in unpaid bills.

By January of 1983, we were unable to keep going and went into liquidation. One co-op survived – making wooden toys and other goods, mainly for the educational company EJ Arnold. It was a painful ending, though, of course, much was learned. However, almost all our young trainees, at a time when Hartlepool's level of youth unemployment was well above 75%, found jobs.

RESPOND!

One of the projects which emerged in the early 1980s became known as *Respond!*. I had become senior chaplain of Teesside Industrial Mission in 1982 and the first big thing I had to organise that autumn was a visit of Church leaders to ICI. ICI's Wilton site had suffered huge losses and there was talk of closure. The visit was followed by a second event, in December 1982, this time also involving senior trade unionists and county councillors from Cleveland. They commissioned us to produce a report on *The Role and Response of the Church to Cleveland's Industrial Crisis*. This led on to the formation, some months later, of *Respond!*, later described by a General Synod member and educationalist as "one of the best adult education projects I have ever seen". Its work was to mobilise the Churches and others to engage with the issues of unemployment and deindustrialisation across Teesside.

GOD'S ACTIVITY IN THE WORLD

A decade on, I was working in Church House, Westminster (1985 – 91) as Secretary to the Church of England's Industrial and Economic Affairs Committee. We were living in south east London, where, one October morning, we awoke to an unimaginable scene.

The date: Friday October 16 1987. The place: South London. Howling winds and crashing windows. Dustbins danced down the street. Heaving branches creaked and swayed as the fiercest hurricane in living memory cut a swathe of destruction across southern England. It was, of course, the great hurricane, wreaking havoc across the capital and far beyond, blocking roads with fallen trees and tearing roofs off houses as people sleep. Such was the scale of the damage that we were amazed so few injuries were sustained or lives lost - thank God.

The following Sunday I was preaching in our local Church. Abandoning the set text, I focused on the Storm.

"What on earth does God think he's playing at?" I began, going on to pose such questions as - what is God doing in the world today? How can we identify his activity, if we are to co-operate with him in our daily lives? No easy answers here. But important questions, nevertheless. For Christians claim to believe in a God who intervenes in history, a God who listens to and answers our prayers, a God who really cares, even for the least of us.

Referring to the Exodus story, I cited the experience of the Children of Israel fleeing Egypt for the safety of Sinai, hotly pursued by a furious Pharoah and angry Egyptian army. God intervened in dramatic fashion, I pointed out, by rolling back the waters of the mighty Red Sea to let the Israelites across, before releasing the floodgates on their unfortunate pursuers.

"And what about Dunkirk?" I continued, reminding the congregation of the escape of British troops from the Normandy beaches in hundreds of small boats, thanks to calm seas and favourable winds - a modern miracle, people have claimed.

Drawing on the theological insights of some of the twentieth century's greatest theological thinkers - Karl Barth, Rudolf Bultmann, Dietrich Bonhoeffer, John Robinson and others - I attempted a potted history of theological thought from the Enlightenment to modern times (and all this in 20 minutes) in order to show how vitally important my opening question was, yet how very complex the issue has become.

A few minutes later, a member of the congregation led the prayers:

"We thank you, Lord, that none of the trees fell on any of the heads of the members of our congregation..."

So: was the Storm an example of God's mysterious hand - or rather puff? Or was it just a natural phenomenon (an Act of God, in insurance parlance)? And how can we know? And does it matter to our faith?

Two weeks later, another god was flexing his muscles and the Stock Market crashed. It could have been Mammon trying to get a word in, or was it God all along, proving his power not only over nature but also over human affairs?

I used the story of my Sermon on the Storm as the basis for another address exactly two years later, in October 1989. I had been asked to speak at the Annual Service of the Cambridge Work Relations Group, the body in Cambridge responsible for managing the Churches' Industrial Mission work in the city. At some stage in the preceding weeks, I had been asked to suggest a title, but had not got round to thinking one up - until receiving a phone call from the organiser, with only ten days to go, reminding me that a title was needed in order to be able to publicise the event.

I must have been in a flippant mood that day. "How about *High Noon for High Tech - God's Judgement on Cambridge*?" I joked, and, to my horror, that was what appeared in the local paper advertising the service.

It was one of the hardest addresses I have ever had to prepare. But I had some specific ideas about what I wanted to tackle. These were the crucial questions:

• Does God really intervene in human affairs?
• How do we understand God's activity in the world today?
• Is God actively promoting the new technologies being researched and developed in Cambridge?
• Is the prosperity of Cambridge a sign of God's blessing?

In case anyone should fail to understand the seriousness of these questions, I focused them on prayer. What do we think we are doing when we pray? What kind of answers do we expect? How do we know if God has heard us? What happens if we aren't sure?

I also referred to a passage in the New Testament, that fascinating account in The Acts of the Apostles, chapter 19, where St Paul's preaching rocked the local economy, causing the bottom to fall out of the market for little silver statues of the local goddess, Artemis - and culminating in a riot from which Paul was lucky to escape in one piece.

"If the gospel can so dramatically impinge on the Ephesian economy of Paul's day", I asked, "why not now, on the economy of Cambridge, or the UK, or Europe, or the whole world?" Which is, of course, directly related to that question: How is God at work in the world today?

I reworked this material for a talk in November 1989 in the City of London to the clergy serving there and began with a brief history lesson.

ADDRESS TO THE CITY OF LONDON CLERGY CHAPTER. November 1989

Late 20th century Western Europe is significantly different from most of the rest of the world, in this respect: overtly religious forces are no longer so powerful in our culture. The strongest forces are economic and technological.

Four years ago I spent some time in Lagos; I found there a numinous culture; people expected the supernatural round every corner. Whenever we went anywhere by car, we always prayed first for 'journeying mercies' - and I soon discovered why!

Or, look at the power of religion and faith in a place like Iran. It was like that in Western Europe and still is in parts up to a couple of centuries ago.

Up to the eighteenth century and later, God was known proven by nature (those mysterious, uncontrollable forces of wind and water, earthquake and fire) and revelation (the Holy Scriptures); but from the nineteenth century onwards, research in the natural sciences (Charles Darwin and others), plus enormous leaps forward in 'taming' nature (agriculture first, then industrial development), plus the application of this more open and enquiring approach to the sacred texts themselves (biblical criticism) led to a huge crisis. No longer would the authority of the Church as the official interpreter of truth be accepted universally. The Queen of the sciences had been dethroned.

This was followed by enormous confusion, and Victorian morality was, in a sense, the only way to prevent a collapse of society and all its values (perhaps we are actually seeing the same phenomenon today). The Victorians found it difficult to hold together the demands of their faith and the increasingly complex industrial society they were developing - hence the privatisation of faith, which still affects the way we live and view the world. That allows nature to be developed and exploited in a separate 'compartment' to faith and morality.

By the end of the nineteenth century, people were perhaps feeling more confident. The fruits of industrial progress were self evident, and no one doubted that God was an Englishman, and things were moving generally in the direction of His Kingdom. But then came the First World War; two great Christian nations slaughtering one another on the battlefields of Europe, the heart of civilisation. This led to a drastic loss of faith and confidence. Somehow the dreadful power of sin had undermined all people's hopes and expectations.

This was followed by the rise of Nazism, and in Germany there was no credible Christian theology or witness to respond to Adolf Hitler, no understanding of how to interpret events, partly because the Church taught that the State was autonomous and the Church should therefore not interfere. So, in practise, much of the Church ended up 'baptising' Hitler.

The thinking of some of those Christians who did oppose Hitler people like Barth, Bultmann, Bonhoeffer was brought together in 1963 by John Robinson, when he was Bishop of Woolwich (his book Honest to God became a bestseller). He was wrestling in 1963 with the same question I am trying to address: How is God at work in the world today?
The meaning of Christianity is pretty important in relation to evangelism and mission, and they only make sense if we expect God to be active and at work changing the world ... So, twenty six years after Honest to God, the same questions - what is God doing, and how do we recognise his activity? - are still absolutely vital, and not adequately being answered.

How do we know what God is doing in the world today? Is he at work through the technological forces and developments which so shape our lives? If he is not, what does that mean about his Lordship? If he is, then how can we co operate with him in order to enable that Lordship to be more fully realised? How is God at work in the world today especially in the area of finance, the creation of wealth, technological development and change. So, what has to be done? Here are three clues:

First, we must recognise the different languages that finance, technology and business use, when compared with the language of faith and ethics. How, for example, do you translate 'share price', 'profit and loss forecast', or the 'FT Share Index' into concepts of love, forgiveness or reconciliation? There is still a crucial task to be done of really bringing these two languages, thought forms, modes of interpreting the world, into creative interaction; this is especially relevant at the present time with all the discussion about the European Monetary System and Exchange Rate Mechanism ... most people probably haven't got a clue about what these technical terms really mean ... and yet they are causing major changes in national and international relationships.

Secondly, the separation of finance, business and technology from morality means that technology can say "I can, therefore I will..", and the only collective constraint is financial; can I afford it, and will it be profitable? So, in effect, we have surrendered to mammon without even a fight! I'm not saying that technology or finance are evil, just that they, like everything else in God's good creation, belong to God and should serve the ends that God wishes. More of this in a moment.

Thirdly, with the dethroning of theology as the Queen of the Sciences, and the consequent loss of authority of the Church as the accepted interpreter of truth, I believe that we have now to find another way of bringing about a Christ inspired society. It may be more modest than in past times, but in the long run could prove more effective. It is based on the resurrection of Jesus Christ, which is God's vindication of the life Jesus lived in what he said and did he made God accessible to ordinary people, gave them clues with which to discover God's will for themselves, taught them, healed them, tore into the Pharisees who burdened them with religious rules and regulations a life which led to the death he died, on the cross. The resurrection, therefore, shows us clearly where our priorities should lie - not in religious observances (God doesn't care two hoots about ceremonial without substance), nor in the observing of laws and rules (what a turn off concept 'morality' seems to have become), not even in the maintenance of the Church, except insofar as it really enables us to be Jesus, but in the living of the life of Christ in all departments of our lives, especially those parts into which so much of our creative energy and ideas is poured our working lives, where it is also the most difficult place to be consistent in doing God's will (Colossians 2).

So what are the key issues likely to be?

Take some examples:

• Is recent legislation counter-productive in relation to the main activities of the City? Look at the degree of governmental and quasi-governmental regulation of the City;
• Subjects such as Third World debt, projects of doubtful environmental value, exploitation of people;
• policies of lending and investing, bearing in mind the responsibilities of the financial institutions to those who have placed and deposited funds with them;
• Executive stress and the question of whether City people are being too greedy for rewards for their work.

What about 'ministry' issues?

• 'Equipping the saints for their work in the world': the ministry of support and encouragement of Christians, which needs to be done at both ends of the commuter line (lay formation and training);
• Getting to know the City institutions - by visiting them and meeting people at all levels; engaging in industrial chaplaincy-type work. This would require careful identification of where

to visit, how to visit, how often to visit, and who to do the visits (this could involve many City clergy and ministers on a part-time basis, but proper training would be essential, with clear aims and a real commitment);

• Working with people, groups, company chairmen and others in the City, on such urgent issues as international debt; the potential effects of the Single European Act (1992); Docklands developments (such as Canary Wharf); mergers and takeovers; the roles and responsibilities of shareholders, individual and institutional; ethical investment; business ethics, Government regulations, codes of conduct and so on;

• A proper pastoral ministry among people working in the City, through prayer, services, counselling, and the full range of good pastoral and evangelistic ministry.

INVOLVEMENT IN AFGHANISTAN

Nearly two decades later, in July 2009, I used the story of Paul in Ephesus in a sermon as a way into a controversial subject – should the British be involved in Afghanistan? The years of chaos in Afghanistan had climaxed with the American-led invasion in 2001 to rid the country – to rid the world – of Al-Qaida and the Taliban, to win once and for all the war against terror.

But it was not to be. And eight years later, with the Taliban re-formed and once again on the rise despite the best military endeavours of over thirty of the world's nations, I preached in my Church, St Michael's Woburn Sands, on this very subject. Paul's message had made a huge impact on the Ephesian economy, I said. Should the message of the Gospel not be speaking to us, forming our 'Christian mind', on the right way forward in Afghanistan?

I was not speaking entirely out of ignorance. Since 2005, I have been closely involved with Afghan Action, a small carpet factory and training school for young men and women in south west Kabul. I have made six visits to Afghanistan and know from experience how difficult it is to do anything in that war torn, chaotic but wonderful country. At our peak in mid 2008, Afghan Action had 174 employees and had trained over 330 young people to weave carpets and read and write. The economic downturn, which really started to bite from mid-2008 onwards, forced us reluctantly to cut back. But we survived and gradually started to grow again, whilst also diversifying into other areas, with training in sewing and tailoring (since mid 2011) now the main thrust of our work.

So I asked the congregation this question: how should we form a 'Christian mind' on the issue of British involvement in Afghanistan? How do we think 'Christianly'? How do we speak about matters of such complexity – but such significance – as British lives are lost, and also the lives of hundreds of young men who, in many cases, fight for the Taliban because they pay better than anyone else and, in some cases, see the Western Forces as enemy occupiers rather than liberators? And then there are the civilian casualties - men, women and children who happen to be in the wrong place at the wrong time.

"Let me remind you," I said, "of the criteria for a Just War, first formulated by St Augustine 1500 years ago, refined by St Thomas Aquinas 1000 years ago and developed and applied – with varying degrees of success – ever since".

I then continued to list and comment on them:

• Is war a last resort after all other non-violent means have been explored? And is it necessary to prevent greater evil and wrong being done? Well, possibly. Though I find the current line taken by our Prime Minister Brown and President Obama unconvincing - that we have to engage militarily over there to prevent terrorist attacks over here. Surely, spending this amount on aid, trade, economic development, education and healthcare would have a far greater impact in Afghanistan and make people far less likely to want to join the Taliban or Al-Qaida?

• Can it be confined to the representatives, ie the armies, and not harm civilians and innocent people directly? Answer: clearly no.

• Is there a reasonable chance of success? This is becoming a serious question and will, undoubtedly, be a major issue in the forthcoming British General Election (due by June 2010).

• Will it, therefore, in the longer term bring peace to the world? For every civilian death, another family despises the West, the invader, the infidel. We have to change that perception.

• Is the violence used and the destruction wreaked proportional to the injury suffered? States are prohibited from using force not necessary to attain the limited objective of addressing the injury suffered. There is now no way of measuring this. The situation is, to put it bluntly, out of control. And we cannot go on like this.

This is what theologians, or teachers of the Church down the ages, have called the Just War Theory. It is difficult to apply. But it is a better starting point than most of the rhetoric from our political leaders about why British soldiers are in Afghanistan and what we think they are doing there.

My involvement in Afghanistan has mainly been focused on social and economic development and, increasingly, education. I would like Britain to be seen by Afghan people as a friend, a supporter and an honest and generous partner. Sad to say, in Afghanistan, too many people see us only as an occupying force. They reluctantly accept that it may better than having the Taliban back in power, but there is little enthusiasm for us. And their present circumstances are desperate and getting worse, with endemic corruption, violence and danger, widespread poverty and unemployment and environmental catastrophe in some areas.

With the end of Western military engagement now drawing near, our hope is that things really will change for the better.

CHAPTER 4

EVANGELISM AND MISSION

In the autumn of 1988 I was invited to speak at a conference for lay people being held in Portsmouth Anglican Cathedral on *Evangelising the Structures*.

My slot was in the afternoon, after a well known national speaker, Bishop Gavin Reid, had given the morning address on *Evangelising Individuals*. I travelled down by train and, on arrival at Portsmouth Station, happened to overhear another traveller being offered a lift to the Cathedral - so I asked for a ride. It was an interesting journey. I sat in the back and no one spoke to me, even to ask why I wanted a ride! On arrival, they got out – and went in – without a glance back to see if I was following.

I was struck by my unwanted sense of anonymity – or rather invisibility.

I told this story at the national conference of an organisation I was involved in setting up in 1989, Linking Up Inter-Faith, to work across the country in inner city areas on urban regeneration. The Conference was held in Manchester in May 1990 and I was one of the speakers.

In my address, I compared my rather trivial experience in Portsmouth with that of so many people who, in their daily lives, feel invisible and quite ignored. "Even though we are going in the same direction and are fellow travellers, we are not sure whether or not the people we are travelling with have recognised that we exist or that what we have might be worth hearing about and listening to or receiving. The role of the Churches with regard to community enterprise and economic initiatives is absolutely crucial in respect to this listening and hearing..".

In the course of my address, I gave a brief history of Linking Up and how and why it had all started. At that stage, I didn't know that, a couple of years later, because of Linking Up, I would be asked to go on secondment to the Government and set up the Inner Cities Religious Council, which was to become the first serious foray by the British Government into matters of faith and practise – beyond its traditional involvement with the Established Church.

The thinking I developed for this address - *Why should Churches get involved in community economic development*? - has proved formative for me ever since.

ADDRESS AT NATIONAL CONFERENCE OF LINKING UP INTER-FAITH May 1990

One of the things I've heard repeatedly over the past few years about the work of the Church in inner city areas, in Council estates, in urban priority areas, is that "at least we are still there". The very presence of the Church in a difficult area where not many people attend is felt to be essential. But then comes the question – even if we are still there, what are we doing? And that raises more questions about the content of the message. Immediately we come up against two problems.

The first is this. There is a collective folk memory, a collective subconscious, of many people in this country who associate religious language, religious symbols and religious buildings with the squire, the factory owner, oppression, exploitation. It is interesting that by the mid 19th century the working classes in this country were already thoroughly alienated from the Churches of all denominations.

A census of Church attendance was held in March 1851, carried out by Horace Mann, a voluntary count of all the people who were worshipping morning and evening in the Churches of England and Wales.. Much to the amazement of the Victorians, out of a population of 18 million people, only 7 million were to be found in Church. The Victorians were shocked - they had thought Britain was a Christian country and that everybody was Christian.

Horace Mann, the organiser, concluded: "It is not difficult to indicate to what particular class of the community this portion of 7 million in the main belongs. The middle classes have augmented rather than diminished their devotional sentiment.. the upper classes too.. But while the labouring myriads of our country have been multiplying.. it cannot be stated that a corresponding increase has occurred in the attendance of this class"...

The second big historical problem that the Churches in urban priority areas have to take seriously is the fact that many, if not most, communities in urban priority areas (UPAs) are now made up of a whole variety of people from different cultures, religions and backgrounds. Christians in this country have perhaps not yet come to terms with the fact that we are neither a secular nor a Christian nation - there are a whole range of different faiths, cultures and beliefs and ideologies in our communities.

We are about to launch into a Decade of Evangelism and I have heard nobody say clearly that if we are serious about having such a Decade we need to understand that not everyone is a blank sheet waiting to be Christianised. There are many different faiths and cultures in our country - so this whole question of Evangelism needs to be unpacked in that light...

I talked about the split between 'secular' and 'spiritual', and how Christians and Churches cope with the apparent indifference to so much of what we are trying to offer. I then referred to my own experience of serving in West Leeds in the late 1970s:

When I was a curate in Leeds, in the next parish to Armley Gaol, we lived on a council estate with a Church built 15 years previously on red shale – which had collapsed after 10 years and had had to be rebuilt. The congregation was tiny – 12 people – and the Church had been in the red from day one... We quickly discovered that the Church on the estate was the only community resource available for people to use. So we opened it up and soon discovered that people were prepared to pay for activities there. And that way, we gradually moved back into financial viability. Then we tried to share effective management of the Church building by forming a group that jointly represented the community as well as the Church.

The week after we left (we moved to Hartlepool in the summer of 1979), the Church council met and reversed all the decisions we had taken, which was rather sad. We had built into the structure a guarantee that the community would have some kind of say over the sort of rents being fixed for the various activities taking place… which lasted for a while. On reflection, I realised how important it is to get the structures right. And how naive I had been!

So how can positive change ever take place? I tried to reflect on the power and influence of the structures within which we seek to live and work, referring to the comment of an American Professor of Business Ethics, Henry Clark, who was to spend six months with me at the Board for Social Responsibility, studying the work of the BSR and Industrial Mission:

"I hear that the Church of England is now the main opposition to the Government in this country", said Henry. I replied: "If that's the case, then heaven help us, because we have no theology of structures". We don't understand structures, those things which so shape our lives.. so we don't expect God to be active and working in and through them.

Henry's book, *The Church under Thatcher* (SPCK 1993), was later to prove a challenging reflection on the work with which I had been involved – and its theological and ideological undergirding.

Back to the history –

Middlesbrough – the 'youngest child of England's enterprise' stands on the south bank of the River Tees. In 1830 it was a hamlet of six houses. Then somebody discovered iron ore in the Cleveland Hills. By 1875 it had a population of 25,000. Interestingly, the first Churches in Middlesbrough were Free Churches. The C of E and the Roman Catholic Church did not establish buildings until the Quakers gave them the money to do so, an example of early ecumenism. There then followed great efforts by the Churches of all denominations in terms of education, health, housing and the alleviation of poverty. There was much emphasis on the morality and immorality of the working classes.

In 1912, a national Church Congress was held in Middlesbrough, chaired by Bishop Gore. Reflecting not only on Middlesbrough, he spoke these prophetic words: "We have confined ourselves to going about relieving misery but we have ignored the growth of industry and the startling contrast of wealth and poverty and the deep injustice felt by working people. Now we have nothing to say"...

Moving south from Middlesbrough to Sheffield, I described the birth and early days of Industrial Mission, before moving back north to Hartlepool.

When I was living in Hartlepool, my daughter came home from secondary school one day and said that the class had been discussing what the pupils wanted to do when they left school. In a class of 30, half of them said they expected to go on the dole. I went to Hartlepool in 1979, and one of the main reasons for wanting to go was because I wanted to solve the problem of unemployment – at that time Hartlepool had the highest unemployment in mainland Britain, 14.5%. Five years later, when we left Hartlepool, it was 25%! ..

At the very least, we can say this: if it's true that economic forces are among the main determining factors in all our lives, then for the Church not to address such powerful forces, not to take them seriously, is tantamount to blasphemy – it's certainly missing the point. It's simply surrendering God's world to Mammon and attempting to pluck a few souls out of the fire and pull them to safety in the ark of salvation.

So what do we want to achieve? Government and the private sector love the idea of self-reliance. It's also a popular concept with people working in third world development, though very often the lessons that might be learned from the developing world don't get applied back here. In some ways it's surprising that it has been the Conservative Governments of the last 10 years that have helped us to see the relationship between poverty and dependency in our own back yard. For me, self-reliance smacks too much of independence and going it alone. All too often in urban priority areas it has actually been 'getting up and getting out' for those who are able to do so.

Perhaps a better concept would be self determination. In other words, a group of people in a local community having some power and control over their own lives but recognising that what they do is not solely up to them. All of us are in inter-dependent relationships with other people and communities and we all need one another.

So, self determination as a goal for communities in urban priority areas might allow the Church to acknowledge that God actually wants to speak to us through the poor.

Almost finally, I asked why the Churches should be involved in community enterprise and economic regeneration, concluding that to address the economic dimension of our lives might be a key to unlocking the door to the problems of poverty, dependence and despair, so prevalent in urban priority areas. The Gospel ought to be the key to identifying the signs and presence of joy, hope, courage, sacrifice, commitment, stickability and perseverance in urban priority areas because these qualities are vehicles for change.

I finished by describing the birth and development of Linking Up and outlined an approach which I have since developed into a training programme, *Catalytic Converters*:

• Paint the picture (gather information, statistical and anecdotal, to understand the context);
• Identify available resources (human, financial, premises etc).
• Clarify the particular problems and opportunities to be addressed as priorities;
• Finally, create an action plan;
• And get on with it.

Churches, I concluded, are actually well placed to follow this process because our members come from a wide range of backgrounds and situations. If we are imaginative, able to listen, prepared to work with people from outside our immediate community and then willing to get on with it, we'll be part of that great movement which is called to change the world!

CHAPTER 5
INDUSTRIAL MISSION

I have spent most of my adult life working on issues related to faith and economic life. I wish there were a definitive history and theological analysis of Industrial Mission (IM) in Britain. The idea has been often mooted and there have been a number of PhDs and, of course, countless articles and papers written about IM. IM has been referred to in many books but, until fairly recently, no one had ever written a detailed and well researched book about IM to compare with the famous book by Ted Wickham, *Church and People in an Industrial City* (Lutterworth 1957).

Malcolm Brown and Paul Ballard have, therefore, done significant work for IM and the Church in publishing *The Church and Economic Life. A documentary study: 1945 to the present* (Epworth 2006). And, in 2010, Malcolm Torry, an industrial chaplain for many years with the South London Industrial Mission and my parish priest when we lived in Charlton, produced a helpful account of workplace chaplaincy over the past 60 years, though it barely scratches the surface of the more comprehensive work of engagement with industry and economy (*Bridgebuilders. Workplace Chaplaincy – A History*. Canterbury Press 2010).

The consequence is that, when histories of Church and society in the 20th century are written, authors have tended to refer back to Wickham but make little reference to work developed since then. More seriously, the significance of theological thinking developed by IM practitioners has been neglected and, at a time when a new generation of serious thinkers are exploring ways of 'being Church' and witnessing to the Gospel, they are largely unaware of the risky, dangerous and challenging experience of being engaged in mission on the margins, which is what the IM tradition represents.

An important theological analysis of Industrial Mission was published in 2011, written by two of IM's longest serving practitioners, Mike West and Peter Cope. This will help to fill some more of the gaps. *Engaging Mission. The lasting value of Industrial Mission for today* (Grosvenor House Publishing 2011) states that, "In the second half of the twentieth century the Christian Churches in Britain undertook together their largest single outreach programme. It.. became known universally as Industrial Mission".

I was Secretary to the Church of England's Industrial and Economic Affairs Committee between 1985 and 1991 and, in that role, worked across the country with Industrial Mission teams. There were at that time over 400 full- and part-time industrial chaplains in Britain. Part of my work involved linking with IM in other parts of the world. In 1985 I spent a month with the Lagos Industrial Mission in Nigeria. In the early 1990s I was part of a pan-European group working on transnational corporations. In 1990, I visited the USA to look at local economic development (what we now call social enterprises) and took part in a conference in San Francisco on business ethics. My report, *Mainstream and Marginal*, was published by the Board for Social Responsibility.

My most significant work in relation to IM was to serve as secretary to the working party, chaired by the Bishop of Kingston, Peter Selby, which reviewed Industrial Mission (1988 – 90) and produced the report *IM - An Appraisal*.

I drafted the 130 page report, but the most significant section was not actually written by me, but by Peter. I reproduce it here, because it states so clearly a dilemma I have struggled with throughout my personal mission and ministry for the past three decades – how do we speak meaningfully of God?

> IM was born of a determination to speak of God outside the familiar setting of Church and parish, and yet in the event its practitioners have often found themselves apparently forced to choose between not speaking of God at all and speaking of God

in slogans imported into the world from the spheres of preaching or academic theology. Keep silent about God, and before long the question will arise about the meaning and purpose of your missionary activity. Speak about God as the Church speaks about God, and very soon, especially in the searching environment of the workplace, the problems of that language will become all too evident. (*IM – An Appraisal. The Church's Response to the Changing Industrial and Economic Order.* Published 1988 by the General Synod Board for Social Responsibility. Second Edition 1989, p.49).

The report used for its sources the historians, apologists and critics of Industrial Mission and the working party made a number of visits to IM teams around the country. The report described four 'generations' of Industrial Mission, which were pertinent up to the early 1990s (the Churches, faced with serious resource problems and a loss of confidence in the public arena, have since pulled back substantially from this pioneer ministry, choosing to concentrate more on parish and congregational ministry, so no longer funding many of the IM posts which had previously existed). The description of 'generations' was coined by one of the great thinkers in Industrial Mission, Mostyn Davies, who worked in Peterborough for over 20 years.

First generation IM, from the 1940s onwards, was about reaching the working classes and mobilising the enormous but untapped potential of the laity. Serious and sustained engagement in and with industry was to lead on to 'generation 2', a real involvement in the humanising of industry through industrial relations projects and organisational development techniques. Two key theological themes were reconciliation and service. This approach prevailed through the 1960s and most of the 1970s and was undergirded by a vision that IM could influence - and christianise - the workplace, and therefore the economy, and therefore society, and therefore the world.

There was also a sustained and serious search for a language which could speak of Christian truth in words which were meaningful to people in the world of work.

'Generation 3' developed in response to the collapse of industry in the 1980s. The changes were so enormous and drastic that people found it difficult to come to terms with them. With massive unemployment and huge upheaval in the whole world of work, the old consensus - in which we all thought we were working in the same general direction for the common good - was shattered. Inefficiency was pilloried, trade unions were demonised, and tired old British society was overhauled in a way no one would have predicted. This was the era of Thatcherism, the era of fragmentation. Old, familiar ways of working for IM disappeared as the industries the chaplains had been involved with were swept away.

IM responded in two ways: first, the skills which chaplains had acquired in industry were, in many places, now brought to bear on unemployment. Projects and initiatives sprung up, increasingly funded through the Government's Manpower Services Commission, itself chaired by Richard O'Brien, a keen Anglican and later to become the Chairman of the Archbishop of Canterbury's Commission on Urban Priority Areas, which produced in 1985 the report *Faith in the City*.

The vision now was of creating 'signs of the Kingdom', building a workplace which affirmed those principles of reconciliation, humanisation and service. And alongside the multitude of local projects which were being set up, a national organisation to support them was created, Church Action with the Unemployed. This had a mainly pragmatic approach, unlike Church Action on Poverty, created at around the same time, which addressed policy issues and has become a significant lobbying organisation. Both these bodies were founded in the 1980s with strong IM inspiration and involvement. They later merged.

Secondly, IM was going through a major theological upheaval. Involvement in the steel strike of 1980 and more so in the miners' dispute of 1984/5 meant standing alongside, organising collections and support for strikers and their families, but also still visiting those at work - and negotiating informally with both sides of the dispute. Through the work of IM in Scotland and Wales with the National Union of Mineworkers and Coal Board management, a resolution to the dispute was actually found, but rejected by the Coal Board Chairman - at the behest of his political mistress.

But what about the rest of industry? Huge redundancies, layoffs, closures, and all around, depression and despair. Where did IM stand? Whose side were we on? Should we be aligned or non-aligned? Should our work be determined by an 'option for the poor'? And if so, how?

More clearly now than ever, IM was faced with two models of working for change:

• the gradualist, purposive approach, 'permeating the system' for God and for Good; this was grounded in 'Public Theology', a belief that Christian Faith has something powerful to offer society - reflected in the writings of theologians like John Atherton and Peter Sedgwick as they attempted to come to terms with the market-led agenda of the New Right;

• or, the more radical approach, anti-capitalist, anti-corporatist, focused on the goal of Liberation. This was particularly pertinent as members of the movement travelled to places like South Africa, India and Poland, returning radicalised and politically committed to struggle for a new world order which more truly reflected God's Kingdom of Justice and Love.

The insights of Liberation Theology, the analysis of colleagues in related fields like community development, the views of people working on development issues in the Third World, all shook British IM deeply. And for several years there was a somewhat fruitless debate about whether IM should be 'factory based' or 'issue based', or even 'project based', in the work.

Around 1990, the Government pulled the plug on many Church-based local training and employment projects. Many of IM's great experiments crumbled to dust as policy emphases moved away from temporary employment to training for work, and the funding disappeared.

Now it became clear that a fourth generation had emerged, 'Local economy-based Industrial Mission'. The rationale was based on the fact that, thanks to Mrs Thatcher, everything now had a financial value. Thus housing, health, education and welfare were as much a part of the local economy as the business and commercial sectors. British Society was being shaped by a 'business executive-led' culture of enterprise. We needed, therefore, to understand and be involved with the whole local economy in a much more disciplined and purposeful way.

Henry Clark, the American academic mentioned above who studied British Industrial Mission and other aspects of urban and social responsibility work in the late 1980s and early 1990s, wrote that this 4th generation development was leading to new kinds of partnerships and coalitions, which he called 'area development programmes' (*The Church under Thatcher*, p.85).

He identified as an example an initiative in the London Docklands to get the Churches to work together more coherently in relation to the largest-scale economic regeneration programme in Western Europe. Another example Clark gave was of Linking Up Inter-Faith. I was closely involved in initiating both these programmes and would claim that the style of engagement with them comes out of the mainstream British Industrial Mission tradition.

CHAPTER 6

INTER-FAITH WORK IN GOVERNMENT

It was my own involvement in Linking Up Inter-Faith - and the contact that gave me with Government - which led to my being seconded to the Government, at the request of the Archbishop of Canterbury, George Carey, in January 1992 to set up a multi-faith body, the Inner Cities Religious Council. It was chaired by a Government Minister and its membership was drawn from the Christian, Hindu, Jewish, Muslim and Sikh faith communities in England – those with a 'significant presence' in inner city areas.

In this new situation, I was based in the Department of the Environment (now called Communities and Local Government) and worked across Government and the regions. My approach was directly related to the generations of IM outlined above.

There was the shock tactic of having a clergyman in Government (generation 1) – 'in' but not 'of' was how I used to describe myself! There were opportunities to develop generation 2 work, building links and bridges, bringing people together, working on staff development, team-building etc. I was heavily involved in generation 3 work in developing projects with local faith communities across the country, including a series of regional inter-faith conferences and seminars which made a significant impact in many areas. And I worked with regional offices, local authorities, voluntary groups and others on local economic and social development (generation 4). I was also in a position to contribute to policy development and to critique it, with occasional successes.

Towards the end of my time with the Inner Cities Religious Council, (ICRC), I wrote an article which was published in *World Faiths Encounter*. It described my work with the ICRC and what we hoped it would achieve.

PARTNERSHIPS FOR A CHANGE. PUBLISHED IN
WORLD FAITHS ENCOUNTER – SPECIAL EDITION
ON RELIGION AND DEMOCRACY (Number 8, July
1994)

In the autumn of 1991, there had been 'disturbances' on
depressed housing estates in places like Newcastle and North
Tyneside, which prompted debate about whether they were
caused by deprivation – poverty, unemployment, poor housing –
or depravation – human wickedness.

Whatever the causes of the disturbances, soon after, one of
the Ministers in the Department for the Environment, Robert
Key, whose particular area of responsibility was inner cities,
wrote to the Archbishop urging that Church and Government
should find a better way of working together for the good of
local communities in inner cities and outer housing estates. He
suggested the setting up of an Inner Cities Religious Council,
chaired by a minister, with representation drawn from across the
main faith communities living in inner city and deprived urban
areas in England.

Robert Key.. had been invited to address a meeting of the Urban
Bishops Group at the Church of England's General Synod in
November 1991 and chose that as the opportunity to announce
his discussion with the Archbishop and the proposed setting up
of the Council.

My secondment to act as its secretary began on 1 January 1992,
under Douglas Hollis [a senior civil servant in the Department
and non-stipendiary minister in the Diocese of Chichester].
There were few established DoE links with any faith.. though I
had some good contacts with the Hindu community through
Linking Up. The Home Office proved to be well connected and I
developed a strong and useful working relationship with one of
the community relations consultants, Satish Malik. The Inter-
Faith Network also became a vital contact, and Brian Pearce,

its Director, has acted as a consultant to the Council since its inception..

When we started, Robert Key said the Council should enable 'full and frank discussion' between faith communities and Government to take place on inner city policies and programmes. Members of faith communities responded positively..

For some, the Council is a focal point for regular discussion with Government primarily on policy matters. For others, the very fact that they are there as people of faith, rather than members of ethnic minorities, is significant. It means that now they can begin to access the mysteries of the bureaucratic machinery of central and local government without having to pretend that their faith is not the central defining feature of their lives.

Over the months, we have come to describe our work as having three strands:

• addressing policy issues;
• sharing information and listening to people in local communities;
• encouraging the development of practical local initiatives.

ADDRESSING POLICY ISSUES

So far, the policy issues discussed by the Council have included Youth Unemployment, Housing and Homelessness, Crime and Vandalism and Religious Discrimination. Our method initially was as follows: a paper produced by officials from the appropriate Government department was circulated to members and then presented by officials and discussed. After the meeting, members consulted with people in their faith communities and fed back their ideas and responses to the paper and points raised. At the next meeting, a Minister from the appropriate department came to the Council to respond..

By the time we reached our third policy issue, Crime and Vandalism, we realised that that model had its difficulties!

Consulting within faith communities was proving difficult, and, in particular, the volume of paper was a problem, so we have been reviewing the process to streamline it. The important lesson being learned is that consultation is not straightforward! Language, culture, education and many other factors need to be taken into account and our hope is that Government is becoming more sensitive in this respect.

At the second Council meeting, in December 1992, members had expressed their concern at the changed arrangements for one of the Government's inner city programmes, the Urban Programme. This had been administered through local authorities, and, as part of its remit, had been able to provide voluntary organisations with funding for what were, often, small scale, but very useful, local projects – a training resource centre for a local Hindu Temple, for example, or an outreach worker involved with glue sniffers or drug addicts. Over the ensuing months, Council members and many people from faith communities and voluntary organisations continued to ask for programmes which would be people-centred. I believe that, in the new arrangements for integrated Government regional offices and a Single Regeneration Budget (announced in Parliament in November 1993), the voices of the faith communities and others have been taken into account.

SHARING INFORMATION AND LISTENING TO PEOPLE IN FAITH COMMUNITIES

The Council decided, at its first formal meeting, to hold a series of Regional Multi-Faith Conferences on Inner Cities. So far, six regional conferences have been held: in West Yorkshire (October 1992); Hull (March 1993); West Midlands (June 1993); South London (October 1993); Greater Manchester (February 1994) and East Midlands (May 1994). Here are some examples of what has been coming out of these conferences:

• From the West Yorkshire Conference, a Bradford Inner Cities Religious Council has been formed and is doing a joint audit of the City; in Batley, the local mosque and church have become actively involved with City Challenge; in Wakefield, meetings between Christians and Muslims, also involving the local authority, have been taking place. A local Inner Cities Religious Council has been formed and a housing initiative is being developed.

• From the Hull Conference, an Inter-Faith Forum has been established.

• From the West Midlands Conference, Wolverhampton Baptist Church/Asian Christian Fellowship has made a bid to City Challenge and the local authority for project funding, and a Hindu Action-Research Project in the Black Country, funded by the Government's City Action Team, has been set up.

• From the South London, Greater Manchester and East Midlands Conferences, multi-faith groups from each area involved are being set up. We hope that they will form a good basis for getting faith communities involved in the bidding arrangements and strategic thinking about the new Single Regeneration Budget in the coming years.

Ministers, in their capacity as Chairman of the Council, have also made visits to local groups and initiatives in such places as Birmingham, Bradford, Gateshead, Leicester, Liverpool, London, Manchester and Stoke on Trent.

The Leicester link is interesting: in February 1993, Robin Squire [the second Chairman of the ICRC, after Robert Key] met leaders and representatives of the faith communities in Leicester and one of the points made to him was that training would help to involve the faiths more effectively in the life of the city. I contacted the local City Challenge team to see if they could help. They suggested that faith communities might like to nominate participants for a pilot Community Entrepreneurs training programme.. At a subsequent visit to Leicester in May, Robin Squire again spoke with faith community representatives about this and in November, Tony Baldry, now chairing the

Council, launched a programme, in which 6 members of local faith communities are participating (out of 9 people recruited so far). The programme involves a year's tailored training and consultancy and Muslim, Hindu and Christian communities are involved. British Telecom, who are providing 50% of the funding, are interested in replicating Community Entrepreneurs programmes in other City Challenge areas, and Bolton has already agreed to run a programme, which has just started.

PRACTICAL INITIATIVES

What we try and do is think strategically about the practical initiatives with which we might be involved. Obviously we try to respond positively to whoever might approach us, at the minimum by linking them with local officials or other agencies who may be able to help.

We are always on the lookout for things which can be adapted or replicated elsewhere, or which can be further developed over time. The Hindu Action-Research Project in the Black Country might, for example, be further developed if funding could be obtained for a Hindu Development Worker across the West Midlands, linking with Hindu communities and helping open up temples and other resources for community use.

We are also in discussion with several faith communities and local authorities about Community Care contracts – how best can local faith communities gain access to funding from social services for targeted provision for their frail elderly members, or for people with special needs? Liverpool Mosque, for example, runs a meals on wheels service for elderly Muslims, with a contract from the local authority to do so.

A FOURTH STRAND: MULTI-FAITH CELEBRATIONS

There is a valuable new development which builds on the local links that have been established. The Council has agreed to initiate Multi-Faith Celebrations in a number of areas during July 1994, working with local faith communities, local authorities, Government departments and agencies and Training & Enterprise Councils. The focus will be young people, and the aim will be to enable people to celebrate their city together and build new friendships across faiths, races and geographical areas. Birmingham, Bolton, Coventry, Derby and South London are now engaged in preparations for activities beginning in early July.

STRATEGY

Over the first 2 years, our strategy has been to concentrate on establishing the Council and becoming known to local faith communities in inner city and deprived urban areas. Our intention is to visit or hold regional Conferences or events covering most of those local authority areas in England. From the conferences held so far, we estimate that new multi-faith activity is developing in at least fifteen areas where nothing much existed before. This is very exciting, but the faiths will need to give thought to how such energy and enthusiasm can be sustained.

As well as linking with local faith communities and inter-faith networks, we have been developing our range of contacts with Government departments and programmes at national and regional levels, especially those with an inner city focus, and also Training & Enterprise Councils, local authorities and the private and voluntary sectors.

These will be important when, over the next few months, we work with faith communities on the new arrangements for integrated Government regional offices.

LOOKING AHEAD

It is still less than two years since the Inner Cities Religious Council had its first formal meeting. It will now wish to build on what has been achieved to date, so that it can make a distinctive contribution to the regeneration (itself a profoundly religious word!) of our inner cities and beyond. Government cannot, for obvious reasons, give the faiths a fast track to changing policies. However, a chance to listen has been provided – and such listening needs to take place on both sides. My own view is that a window of opportunity has opened and much is to be gained by both Government and faiths, for the benefit of the whole of society.

On a personal note, I have enjoyed my secondment and have learned a great deal from all those with whom I have worked, in Government, in faith communities and elsewhere. My colleagues Jayne Fullwood and David Nixon are DoE officials working full time with me. Their contribution to the work - and that of countless other officials centrally and around the country - has helped to get faith more firmly onto the agenda of Government. I continue to be disappointed that faith communities seem to give so little support to their members working in difficult jobs, in Government and elsewhere. If discipleship can in any sense be measured by degrees of time and commitment, then what people of faith who are civil servants do in their working lives needs to be affirmed as service and supported, challenged and resourced accordingly by the leaders and pastors of their faith communities.

Given the current debate about the lack of shared values in our society, the contribution of faith in this whole area should be of paramount importance. I believe that the Inner Cities Religious Council is one significant way in which the faiths themselves can develop a new understanding of each other and a new impetus to work together; I also believe that the Government is receptive to what the faiths have to offer the nation. It cannot always be a tidy relationship; there will be heartache at times and no doubt much heart searching. But we have it, and it is working – so let it be used and let it become a distinctive and special instrument for good.

In the late summer of 1994, I was succeeded at the ICRC by David Randolph-Horn, an Anglican parish priest from Aston. His work helped to sustain and consolidate the work of the Council and when he moved to Leeds – where his work on inter-faith issues broke new and important ground – he was followed by another Anglican clergyman, David Rayner. During his time, the Council's work was 'mainstreamed' in Government and the number of officials working on faith issues grew substantially.

CHAPTER 7

UNEMPLOYMENT AND THE FUTURE OF WORK

In September 1994, we moved north again, to set up a new ecumenical organisation across North East England, The Churches' Regional Commission in the North East. This was the brainchild of a dynamic group of clergy and lay people in the region, headed by Bob Langley. He articulated a model of Church using three overlapping circles: Pastoral, Enabling and Engaging. The Pastoral circle was primarily the responsibility of parishes and congregations; the Enabling circle was the diocesan staff supporting mission and ministry (administration, education etc) and the Engaging circle was the responsibility of Industrial Mission, Social Responsibility and a range of other Church ministries and agencies working 'out there', engaging on social, economic, cultural and environmental and other issues. My job, then, was to find effective ways through which to support, resource, co-ordinate and encourage the Engaging ministries.

During 1995 and 1996, a working party set up by Bishop David Sheppard toured the country to explore with a wide range of people the theme of *Unemployment and the Future of Work*. Chaired by Patrick Coldstream, the secretary was Andrew Britton, former head of the National Institute for Economic and Social Research - and the group visited North East England in the early spring of 1996. I was responsible for organising their visit and they met with an interesting mix of people, including industrial missioners and Church groups, as well visiting industries and workplaces to talk with people at work. They also met unemployed people convened by *Respond!* in Teesside and explored different ways of understanding employment with the Churches' Arts and Recreation Chaplaincy.

Their report, published in Spring 1997, caused a furore, coming out in the run up to the General Election. Among their recommendations was one which we in the North East were keen to endorse and respond to: to set up an Employment Forum. This we did, forming the North East Employment Forum, which held a major regional event in October 1998. Until 5pm the night before the Forum, Prime Minister Tony Blair was scheduled to speak. But he cried off at the last moment and in his place came Hilary Armstrong, a local MP and, at that time, Housing Minister. She later became the Chief Whip.

In January 1998, we moved back to London, but I continued my involvement with the North East Employment Forum for the next 12 months, visiting the North east frequently.

In 1999, a national charity, Employment Forum UK, was formed, chaired initially by the Bishop of Wolverhampton, Mike Bourke, a member of the *Unemployment and the Future of Work* follow up group. The *Crucible* article which follows was written by Wilf Wilde and myself.

EMPLOYMENT FORUM (UK): ARTICLE IN *CRUCIBLE* May 2003

When the Ecumenical Churches' report on *Unemployment and the Future of Work* was published in April 1997, it was instantly front page news, calling, as it did, for new training provision, a minimum wage, an overhaul of the social security system and "enough good work for everyone". Some saw it as a thinly veiled criticism of the Conservative Government in an election year. Among the recommendations – not spelt out in any detail in the section headed Enough Good Work for Everyone - was a proposal: for a national employment forum. It should have a broad remit, to include not just employers and employees, but consumers, investors, central and local Government, and of course the unemployed. Its role: to focus on employment; jobs and the future of work. It should be broad-based and consensual. It should advise not only Government, but all interested groups (*Unemployment and the Future of Work. An Enquiry for the Churches.*)

The working party responsible for gathering the evidence and producing the report spent several days in North East England during 1996. Their visit was co-ordinated by Rev Chris Beales of the Churches' Regional Commission. Chris had a long history of involvement in employment issues, having been an industrial chaplain in Leeds and Teesside, then Secretary to the Church of England's Industrial and Economic Affairs Committee from 1985 – 91, followed by a period on secondment to the Government's Inner Cities Directorate in the Department of the Environment, where he set up a multi-faith consultative body, the Inner Cities Religious Council (1992 – 94).

His experience of work in some of the country's worst unemployment areas - during the 1980s and 1990s – meant that, when the report was published, he was keen to build on the momentum created and strengthen the Churches' commitment to work in a field which, over recent years, had become less popular and less well resourced by the mainstream denominations. An old Durham University friend with whom he had kept in touch, Dr Wilf Wilde, had contributed ideas and brought his own expertise as a development economist and stockbroker – and radical socialist thinker and lay theologian. Together Chris and Wilf set out their vision for a model of 'missionary' engagement through which the Churches might more strategically address such issues. In a seminal paper produced in 1997, they mapped out a programme for the next few years.

TAKING THE EMPLOYMENT FORUM IDEA FORWARD

So Chris offered to run with the idea of a Forum. The Churches Together in Britain and Ireland (CTBI) steering group gave its blessing – but no money. Employment Forum (UK) was born, with three of the CTBI group forming the Board of what became, in July 1999, a registered charity chaired by the Bishop of Wolverhampton, Mike Bourke. Four years on, Employment Forum (UK) had become a small, innovative and enterprising agency for a new kind of Christian engagement with the nation's economic, political and social life, a 'Christian-led' inter-faith employment and regeneration initiative linking faith communities with a programme of action and research.

Our involvement in particular with Muslim communities has been of profound significance in the light of Nine Eleven (*Faiths and Finance – Principles and Practise. Involving the faiths in community regeneration and development*. Employment Forum (UK) seminar report, November 2001). Likewise, the Black Economic Empowerment Conference in 2002 was the first of its kind in the UK and, in terms of feedback and follow up, highly successful (*It's Time to Move Mountains*. Report of Employment Forum UK's first National Black Economic Empowerment Conference, held in Croydon, April 2002). Our work has brought together members of faith communities with people from Government, public, private and voluntary sectors, and unemployed people to enable new and creative networks to develop, to mobilise people and give them a distinctive voice. We did this initially through regional conferences in East London, the North West and the West Midlands for between 100 – 200 people, piloted first in North East England in October 1998.

This article starts by looking at some of the theological thinking behind our practical actions and reflects at the end on how we have been changed by our experience. It then looks at three case studies on key aspects of our work: on the potential practical role of the Church and faith communities in economic and social regeneration; on our interfaith work; and on our Black Economic Empowerment Programme with black majority Churches. Our broad aim has been to breathe fresh life into the Church and faith communities' engagement with politics and economics. We link employment with social exclusion, poverty and regeneration, with debt and finance, and with regional government and hopes for greater democracy. We have worked to build bridges between people of different faiths and have shown the practical possibilities of working together with shared values and solidarity.

Our theological intention has been to bring Good News. The work was to be incarnational and action-based. We have involved people directly in concerns relating to their daily experiences, and their economic and social circumstances. This approach takes power seriously and seeks to help people to take greater responsibility for and control over their own personal and collective destinies. It does so from a distinctive (but not exclusive) Christian perspective.

We have also tried to take the Church seriously; the Church exists to 'be Jesus' in the world, living faithfully and dangerously in pursuit of justice and love. So we try to reinforce, support and build on what is already happening, and spread models of good practise through our forums and events. Consequently, we have helped Churches and faith communities to act as brokers. After all, they have extensive networks and contacts and can play a pivotal role in bringing together disparate people to explore ideas and make things happen.

It would be easy to get the impression that the Church has little to say about the economic policies and political priorities of our communities and nation; not much to offer, no case to make for things to be changed. Too often, the energies of our clergy are spent trying to defend their posts in the face of threats to cut them. Both national and parish resources have been so pressed by the consequences of Church decline that a 'can't do' culture threatens to take over.

We believe that Employment Forum now has a track record and substantial experience of fund-raising and programme development. Our desire is to engage the Churches in a dialogue - not just about social engagement, or employment, or industrial mission - but about future ways of 'being Church'. It is a practical plea for a Church which stands for an alternative global order to that of the powers that be. Of course we're not alone in doing this – lots of others are deeply involved. But we are unusual in one key respect – we work deliberately across the divides of faith and ethnicity. Hence our substantial engagement with Muslim and other faiths, and our deliberate and well resourced development of a black economic empowerment programme.

FAITH COMMUNITIES AS CATALYSTS FOR REGENERATION

Today's Government is courting the faith communities in ways which five years ago could hardly have been imagined. Faith in the Neighbourhood style initiatives present an opportunity to bring two largely separate – pastoral and industrial - ministries together (See the Inner Cities Council: *Faith in Community* (2002), and the Joseph Rowntree Foundation: *'Faith' in Urban Regeneration*. Also see recent reports by the Local Government Association and the Inter-Faith Network).

The financial plight of many British Churches is now giving rise to considerable concern. Yet the Churches, along with other faith communities, are the largest and most well resourced part of the voluntary sector, though often they do not realise it. Faith communities have a presence in every locality and can open doors to people who otherwise might be excluded.

A key feature of Employment Forum's work has been to encourage the Churches and others to build on these distinctive strengths. We need a 'make-it-happen' culture and a framework enable Churches to imbibe new ways of working, becoming actively involved in local partnerships and more effectively involved in practical regeneration initiatives - not just leaving it to those few people with an interest in these things!

As Church, we are not very good at specifying what we are trying to achieve in the language of Government - outcomes and outputs. So we are often disappointed that our work seems unrecognised, while others receive huge amounts of money for what can appear to be rather limited and unimaginative programmes making little effect on deprivation.

Churches and other faiths have rarely attempted to catalogue their very substantial investment in and commitment to local communities, which often represents a huge potential leverage. In a recent 'Church/Community Audit' in Thamesmead, South East London, for example, the volunteering hours put in by members of 8 local churches were found to amount to over 500 hours/week – 'sweat equity' equivalent to c£100,000 a year. A local directory compiled by Greg Smith, one of the authors of 'Faith' in Urban Regeneration, identified in Newham and Hackney 685 different faith organisations. In Newham alone, 25,000 people are involved with faith-based organisations in different ways.

INTER FAITH WORK

The East London Employment Forum, held at Canary Wharf in November 1999, crystallised our growing work with the Muslim community in particular (*Catalysts for Change: Challenging the Faith Communities of East London* and *The Alphabet Soup of Regeneration*). This report described two seminars for young people under 30 from faith communities in East London, organised by Employment Forum (UK) and held in January and March 2001.

East London is experiencing rapid development - with 150,000 new jobs in the Docklands and a £10 billion infrastructure development. But will it really bring jobs to local people? East London has had an enormous number of local initiatives, where nearly every scheme from New Deal to Employment Zones has been tried. Yet there had been a 50% drop out rate from New Deal in Tower Hamlets and Newham. There is a particular difficulty in managing the benefit/work transition in London because the cost of housing makes people dependent on housing benefit – low waged jobs cannot make rents affordable.

Our joint organisers were unemployed Bangladeshi women graduates based in the Tower Hamlets Graduate Forum, which meant crossing a number of barriers for them – and us. The Forum led onto a project, with funding from ING Barings, to research the reasons for the high level of graduate un- and under-employment (especially among the Bangladeshi community).

Likewise, at a seminar in 2001 for Church leaders in West London, we discovered that 30% of the population in the Borough of Harrow is Asian - but these diverse communities are not yet interacting well within the Church. The East London work also built strong links with Saif Ahmad, Chief Executive of a Muslim Housing Association and, in 2001, founder of a Muslim-led inter-faith regeneration project, Faith Regen (UK). It has gained funding to set up a number of IT information and advice kiosks in London, in mosques, churches and other places of worship, to reach unemployed and socially excluded people, providing information in 8 different languages about training and employment opportunities. Faith Regen has also produced a Faiths' Toolkit for Jobcentre Plus staff and has run an Upskilling Imams training programme, on which we also worked.

A significant contribution the Church of England could make is to take deliberate steps at parish level with a simple training programme to engage in raising awareness of what Muslims believe, what their circumstances are and how we might work effectively with them - a practical way for the Church to respond positively to the critical political situation we face.

FAITHS AND FINANCE

The first *Faiths and Finance* seminar in November 2001, although planned for nearly a year, assumed far greater significance after September 11 than anyone could have predicted. 80 people came together, at the London Central Mosque and Islamic Cultural Centre, London – Christians, Hindus, Jews, Muslims and Sikhs - to discuss local and international issues of faith and finance, principles and practise. One of the key practical issues arising was the need to address ways of exploring and applying Islamic banking and finance principles, based on interest free lending. Malcolm Hayday, now head of the new Charity Bank, spoke about its creation, concerned to back social entrepreneurship, development and community regeneration. The Conference revealed a great sense of shared values and solidarity. Our keynote speaker was Professor Rodney Wilson, of the Durham

University Institute for Middle Eastern and Islamic Studies. His address, subtitled *Challenging the System, Challenging the Faiths*, observed that, in many respects, there were more differences within each of the main Abrahamic religions that there was between them.

IT'S TIME TO MOVE MOUNTAINS

There are over 3000 black majority churches in the UK – and 250,000 adherents. The black Christian churches are one of the fastest growing parts of the UK Church. Whilst only 8-10% of Britain's white population regularly attends church, this rises to 33% in the black community. *It's Time to Move Mountains*, the first National Black Economic Empowerment Conference to be held in the UK, was initiated by Employment Forum in order to raise the profile of the black Christian community. The Conference was held in Croydon, where 25% of the population is of ethnic minority origin; 50% in some parts of the borough. We were told that there are 4 million black and Asian people in Britain today, 7% of the population. 2 million live in London. In 2000, white unemployment was 6.9%; ethnic minority unemployment was 13%. Yet within such broad categories, there is much diversity. Hindus were four times less likely to be unemployed than Pakistanis or Bangladeshis (25% of whom are self-employed). A black Caribbean man earned £115/week less than a white man; the Pakistani man £150 less. Black women earned £30/week more; a Pakistani woman £34 less than a white woman. 45% of Chinese were professionals or managers.

BLACK EMPOWERMENT PROGRAMME

At the Croydon Conference, Rev Ron Nathan, the instigator of our Black Economic Empowerment Programme and closely involved with Employment Forum since its inception, had led the thinking of black church leaders by arguing that "we need to revisit our fundamental ideas about being the church in society (and)… translate our religious language into political language". The strong cultural legacy of focusing on 'the spiritual' - at the expense of engaging in social, political and economic issues in daily life – needed to be addressed".

The Black Economic Empowerment Programme has now gained funding from the Office of the Deputy Prime Minister and the City Parochial Foundation, having received a substantial grant from Lloyds TSB Foundation and the Community Action Network to get going. Regional black economic empowerment events, organised by our Development Director Shola Lana, have tackled enterprise development, training, volunteering, accessing funding and making theological sense of it all. Events have been held in Croydon, Leicester, Nottingham, Manchester, West Yorkshire and Wolverhampton; with more to come in Bristol and Cardiff. In London, through funding from London Excellence, we have been helping to train and develop the work of identified black leaders and social entrepreneurs. The second National Black Economic Empowerment Conference will be held at the end of May 2003.

In many of our forums we have heard of the pitfalls of regeneration spending. Applications are difficult to produce and payment arrangements often undermine financial and job stability. Reporting and monitoring too cause many complaints; risk is often transferred from the public sector purse onto people lower down. The inability of central Government genuinely to give up its nanny state role re-surfaces again and again in our meetings on regeneration. The bidding process can even set communities in competition, with one minority community bidding effectively against another.

FROM THE MAINSTREAM TO THE MARGIN

Employment Forum has always had a bold aim for its missionary and evangelising role within the mainstream Church. We have sought to engage practically and effectively with the politics and economics of the wider society. By focusing on employment and regeneration, however, we seem to have moved away from the 'mainstream' denominations towards urban areas where the black majority Churches and Muslim communities are the dominant expressions of faith. What started as a mainstream focus with a concern for the voiceless has ended up linked with the frequently marginalised and on the edge. This has forced us to attempt to transcend the barriers of race, ethnicity, economic background and belief. In our common endeavour, a belief in God's better rule has been our continuing principle.

We have had much positive support from Bishops and Church leaders for our vision and work. But, somehow, we have found it difficult to gain a hearing in the 'mainstream'. Our relative failure to speak to the mainstream has symbolised for us the struggles of the conventional institutional Church: managing death gracefully has been our experience of too much in Anglicanism and other traditional denominations.

However, this difficulty has not been true of another frequently marginalised community – the black Pentecostal Churches – often based in our inner cities. We have found that working with black majority Churches is having powerful resonance both from them and from the Government – given that most of our present 2003/5 funding is for this area of our work. The common experience of poverty and oppression has provided us with some fascinating dialogue; of a Muslim friend speaking at a black empowerment seminar in Bradford on the need for a wider spiritual renewal; of a Sikh local Government officer running a funding workshop for black Christians; of the black Pentecostals speaking of their faith at the Islamic Cultural Centre during the annual Conference of the National Ecumenical Agency in Further Education.

THE BLACK CHURCHES: A THEOLOGICAL JOURNEY?

Indeed what we have observed within the black majority Churches is a theological journey for some which is opening up the personal Gospel of saving souls for the afterlife to a much broader one of the salvation health of its wider community and of its broader social, political and economic empowerment. This

newly liberating theology – articulated so clearly by Ron Nathan
– is able to draw on traditional black Pentecostal theology
but reflects also the African and Afro-Caribbean experience
of exploitation and deprived, marginalised communities.
Sometimes it emerges as the radical strain to the prosperity
gospel, so powerful to so many poor black communities from the
USA and elsewhere. One senses a generation gap as the second
generation of black British Christians come to term theologically,
politically and economically with their church and community
experience here. The power of the older pastors with the Black
Churches is immense and it is difficult dilemma for the younger
black leaders to know how hard to push within their own
community.

We take some comfort that our move from addressing the
mainstream to working on the margins is echoed both in Jesus'
and Paul's experience.

Maybe identifying more closely and working with Muslims and
other marginalised people in our community – giving but also
receiving - is the new next step of faith for the Church if it is
to stay true to its divine calling. In those traditionally seen as
lacking the 'true' faith, it is indisputable that deep devotion to and
real faith in God exists and is flourishing. We – the People of God
- need and want to be part of that, bringing, we trust, something
of the power and presence of Jesus Christ to an ongoing
engagement which is ultimately about building God's Kingdom.

By early 2005, the work had grown considerably. We were running
programmes across a range of different fields. My son Andy had
joined the team and set up Connect2Employment. A new colleague,
Mike Osbourne, and I were developing work with schools to broker
investment in sports and leisure facilities onto school sites. And the
black economic empowerment work was expanding. A new project
was also emerging after several years of incubation – Afghan Action.

I gave a talk in February 2005 to a construction group called CAPSIG
on the theme of community consultation. I began by summarising

Employment Forum's work:

• Connect2Employment runs a minority ethnic employment
outreach programme in East London, a construction training
programme, English language and basic skills courses and a
recruitment agency specialising in construction, hospitality and
security;
• Employment Forum runs conferences, seminars and training
programmes to mobilise faith communities (of all faiths) to get
stuck into helping people in their neighbourhoods to find work,
get into training, start businesses, develop childcare projects,
support the elderly and disabled.. and much more. We've run
seminars with The Economist on Faiths and Globalisation,
conferences and training events across the country with African
and Caribbean church leaders and members on economic
development and done a lot of work on further education and
training;
• Rainmakers incubates new businesses and provides a mentoring
service for small community organisations, helping them with
needs assessment, business planning and accessing funds.

Among the businesses we're incubating are

• Slipstream Ltd, which builds health, fitness and sports facilities
in Church secondary schools – starting in the north of England;
• NAGODA: the National Gospel Development Agency, which
runs a national black economic empowerment programme
in England and Wales, working mainly with black majority
churches;
• Afghan Action, which is developing a training school for carpet
weavers in Kabul, Afghanistan – the carpets will be imported to
this country and sold here, thus supporting the local economy
back there and creating viable businesses.

I then went on to speak about consultation and illustrated this from
my own experience.

Urban Catalyst is an innovative property developer, expert at brokering relationships between the private and public sectors. I have been involved in several bids for major regeneration projects with Urban Catalyst. We bid together some years ago to develop the Millennium Community in Castleford, West Yorkshire, on the site of an old pit at Allerton Bywater. We did some careful research and in our presentation it was my job to emphasise the need not for another white, working class community but for a mixed community with homes and facilities carefully designed to meet the requirements of the multi-faith, multi-cultural community of the wider sub region. The interviewing panel hadn't thought of this, and we had a bit of a sharp exchange. As we went out, I apologised to my colleagues. But their response was: we won't work with them even if we are short listed. And we were. And they wouldn't.

In Bermondsey Square, near London Bridge, we were more successful. It was a long process, with our consortium eventually getting shortlisted and then getting the contract, subject to all the usual processes. We held a public meeting which had 100 people present and some angry 'over my dead body' exchanges. One of the leading people in the resistance movement, himself an architect, is now very supportive. He actually had some important reservations about the earlier designs, and he and others were carefully listened to – with the eventual design taking account of these points.

We had an elaborate consultation process, involving not only the public meeting but open days for local people to see the design and record their views and interest. We also did two lots of delivering leaflets round the houses. We could have posted them out.. but we thought it'd be better to deliver them and get into conversation on the way round with people. We also targeted shops, church, pubs and community groups to make sure they had the info and knew the score.

It's worth a visit to Bermondsey Square as the development there has been significant and substantial – and very effective. Allerton Bywater is also developing now, though at the time of my CAPSIG talk things were still at a standstill due to the very issues we had raised in our presentation.

CHAPTER 8

AFGHAN ACTION

I worked with Employment Forum UK – which changed its name to Employment Focus in 2004 – until 2006, when I moved to work with the child it had created, Afghan Action. In July 2002, Employment Forum's East London outreach worker, Ilyas Ayoub, introduced me to a group of Afghan refugees. Three years later, a new charity was formed, Afghan Action (originally called the Afghan Training Foundation), and we obtained the funding needed from the British Government to open a small training centre in Kabul, Afghanistan.

Now known as a Training and Business Incubation Centre, we train young people in carpet weaving and sewing and tailoring. We provide education in literacy and numeracy (in Dari), English, ICT and business skills and also provide on-site healthcare and a midday meal. Since 2005, we have trained over 900 people.

We have also run programmes in the UK with Afghan diaspora groups and a major three year programme, *Building Bridges*, completed its work in December 2012. Its aim was to raise awareness about Afghanistan with schools, faith and community groups, businesses and media. We also ran a smaller awareness raising programme with schools in East Yorkshire and did an interesting and ground-breaking study in North London on inter-generational issues in Afghan families.

A more substantial piece about Afghan Action's work will be published in 2014.

I drafted this summary (below) of Afghan Action's work in Afghanistan in July 2011. Since then, things have, of course, developed. We have now trained 24 women to sew and make clothes and uniforms and have 12 of them now working in our premises, with a further 12 newly recruited and 12 young female apprentices just starting. They make clothes, uniforms and quilts – quilts for the internally displaced refugees living in desperate conditions in tent camps around Kabul.

AFGHAN ACTION: THE STORY SO FAR
July 2011

Afghan Action has been running a centre training and employing carpet weavers, young men and women mainly aged 14 to 25, including some disabled people, for nearly seven years in the Karte Se District of Kabul. In July 2011, a new programme training people to sew and make clothes was started and this will train 46 people, mainly women, over a 2 year period.

Literacy and numeracy teaching, on-site healthcare and a nourishing midday meal have always been an integral part of the programme.

The work grew out of contacts made in 2001 with Afghan refugees in East London and our initial thrust (2005–2008) was to train young people and employ many of them. 330 young men and women (including a number of disabled people) took part in the training programme in the first 3 years and, by late 2008, we were employing 180 people, with contracts to supply carpets to Habitat and John Lewis.

Startup funding for Afghan Action came from the UK Government's Department for International Development (DFID) through its Business Linkages Challenge Fund. This was managed on behalf of DFID by Emerging Markets Group (EMG), whose Chief Executive visited Kabul in April 2008 to assess the programme.

Over the past 3 years, 330 people have been trained (216 males and 117 females). It is estimated that about 10% have dropped out of training. Of the remainder, some 80 continue to work in the factory and about 8 are still in training. The majority [who have finished their training are in business now on their own, including about half in carpet weaving from home. In addition, some have continued with their studies while undertaking other work. Of the remaining 115 it is assumed that the majority have returned to their towns and villages with new skills and training. Anecdotally, many have set up carpet weaving operations. Most of these individuals are returning refugees from Pakistan and Iran who had settled temporarily in Kabul's slums.. (EMG Report, June 2008)

From the autumn of 2008 onwards, the economic downturn began to bite and had a serious effect on Afghan Action's sales, forcing painful cutbacks in carpet production and the layoff of many employees in Kabul. Since then, the work has gradually rebuilt and currently there are 65 people on site employed or in training and 60 people working at home developing their own weaving businesses, supported by Afghan Action.

In October 2010, a 6 month pilot programme, T2GO, was launched, taking 12 trainees to a further stage of development, learning English, ICT skills and business skills, in order to equip them for starting and running their own business(es). Afghan Action decided at this time to rebrand its work in Kabul as a Training and Business Incubation Centre. All trainees - carpet weavers and tailors - undertake a 12 month programme of vocational skills training and education, on completion of which they move into employment, set up their own business or continue in education.

In June 2011, the Trustees of Afghan Action adopted the proposals of a paper, New Directions for Afghan Action, which had been drafted in full consultation with Afghan colleagues, that Afghan Action's work in Afghanistan be refocused in the following ways:

• Afghan Action in Afghanistan should become a Skills and Enterprise Development Agency and establish Training & Business Incubation Centres in Afghanistan;
• Afghan Action should instigate a programme of market research to identify the particular needs, gaps and opportunities

for local Training & Business Incubation Centres elsewhere in the country, working where possible with other schools and partners, both in Afghanistan and the UK;

• The mixed economy model – of income generating work (through production and sales) and training/education/ healthcare/food paid for or provided through donations and sponsorship should be continued;

• Afghan Action should aim to position itself as a leading agency in Afghanistan in promoting and enabling the development of good jobs, sustainable businesses and fair markets, targeting in particular the SME and social enterprise sectors;

• A national Development Director, based in Afghanistan, should be recruited and appointed to take forward the work in Afghanistan.

During 2012, I developed an idea for expanding our work in Afghanistan. I used the term 'bolt on' as shorthand to describe what could be done – bolt on to an existing secondary school a vocational skills training programme for, say, 2 – 3 hours per day after pupils had completed their academic studies.

CHAPTER 9

YOUTH UNEMPLOYMENT

Reflecting on the 'bolt on' idea, it struck me that it could also apply in the UK, with nearly one million young people unemployed, despite a serious skills shortage in some areas of the Economy, especially engineering and construction. I drafted an article to describe the ideas and a proposal to address what might be done.

MEASURES FOR REDUCING YOUTH UNEMPLOYMENT December 2012

The statistics speak for themselves. Nearly a million unemployed young people in the UK. Many of them are recent graduates, in addition to the 40% (2 in 5) who are in non-graduate jobs (says *The Futuretrack Report*, commissioned by the Higher Education Careers Service Unit). And many more young people are also working in jobs way below their capacity, often part time in the retail or hospitality sectors. A generation of disillusioned young people, their dreams shattered and hopes left unfulfilled.

The picture looks bleak. So many of our youngsters long for work with purpose and meaning – but lack the skills to fill the thousands of well paid, challenging jobs our Economy needs – so those jobs remain unfilled or are taken by people from overseas.

The UK needs to increase by as much as 50% the number of science, technology, engineering and maths (STEM) graduates it is creating, says the Royal Academy of Engineering. 100,000 STEM graduates are needed a year just to maintain the status quo.

There are real, well paid jobs out there, with long term prospects. But where are the people with the skills? And why on earth are we not training and equipping them?

It's not just graduates we need. With the Thames Tideway Tunnel we have one of the world's most ambitious water tunnelling programmes – and can't find the home-grown labour. In fact, in the UK, we are 25,000 tunnelers short.

What possible solutions might there be?

A new kind of school has emerged in the past 5 years which could be a foretaste of positive things to come. University Technical Colleges – UTCs – provide education for 14 to 18 year olds, combining academic studies with technical vocational skills training.

The pioneer UTC is the JCB Academy in Rocester, Staffordshire, which opened in September 2010. Its GCSE and A level results last summer were stunning. The Head Boy and Head Girl were offered places at good universities and turned them down to take up Higher Apprenticeship opportunities in engineering. There are now 33 UTCs either open or due to start in 2013 or 2014, with more to come.

UTCs are State schools and cater for all abilities. They have university support and involve companies and other partners in developing the curriculum, providing work experience and offering technical projects. Being at a UTC is more like being in a workplace than a school. The daily schedule is likely to run from 8.30am to 5.30pm over 40 weeks, broken up into 5 terms of 8 weeks. Real commitment is expected – just like being at work. And the opportunity is there for all to progress into an apprenticeship at 16, or into A levels, or whatever succeeds them, and on to University. The time balance for 14 – 16 year olds is 60% academic and 40% vocational and that balance can be sustained or reversed for the 16 – 18 stage. Of course, smart companies will spot potential employees and be keen to ensure their talents and interests are nurtured.

I am involved in developing a UTC. We submitted our application a month ago and hope we will be invited for interview. I am also involved in work in Afghanistan with a charity, Afghan Action, which set up a Training & Business Incubation Centre seven years ago in Kabul. We educate young men and women aged 14 – 25 and provide healthcare and a midday meal. And we train them to make handmade Afghan carpets and also to sew and make clothes and uniforms. We are a rather unsophisticated version of a UTC!

In thinking about how to expand our work, we came up with a simple idea – to "bolt on" technical vocational skills training and business incubation to existing secondary schools. In Afghanistan, only 1 in 10 secondary school graduates get to University. The country is desperately short of indigenous skills – engineers, IT technicians, managers, administrators, teachers, accountants, book keeper, plumbers, joiners and many more.

So, 2 hours a day of 'bolt on', before or after 3 or 4 hours of academic studies – on a school site – could be a simple and affordable way of helping people acquire the skills the Afghan Economy so desperately needs.

And then I thought – why not do the same in the UK? Most schools can't just convert to UTCs, nor should they. A local centre could offer – for pupils who want it – technical vocational skills training for 2 hours daily after school, supported by local companies, leading to apprenticeships and employment opportunities.

This will not suit everyone. But identifying skills shortages and starting to equip young people - while still at school - with the very skills they need to progress into proper training and find a good job should be tried and tested.

And one more thing. The minimum wage for 16 year old apprentices is £2.65 per hour. For youngsters of the same age in other jobs, it's more than a pound more, £3.68 per hour. What a scandalous disincentive to get good training and a job with real prospects.

To make a serious and lasting impact on youth unemployment,

we should start with school-age pupils and give them the chance to get a taste of real work – including the discipline, the time keeping, the respect for safety, the chores as well as the challenges. With commitment from employers, schools, Government and the wider community, our young people can grow again into a world class workforce with opportunities for work not just at home but across the globe.

So let's test the model – and give our youngsters a future.

ALPHA BUILDING SERVICES AND ENGINEERING

I first became aware of the idea of a University Technical College in 2010, through my involvement with Alpha Building Services and Engineering Ltd in Newham, East London. Based in huge old Thames Water buildings in West Ham (with the oldest beam engine in London), Alpha BSE is an innovative construction training provider run by a highly skilled and experienced entrepreneur, John Budu-Aggrey.

I had met John in 2003 through Newham College as, at the time, I was looking for opportunities to develop construction skills training for unemployed adults in East London. John became a good friend and we worked together to obtain the funding and provide training for over 150 people in the next few years.

Our work together began through the Midtown Foundation, a small, not-for-profit company I had set up whilst working in central London in 1998/99. My fellow directors were Ken Bartlett – who would later become Chair of Employment Forum (UK) and then of Afghan Action – and Ken Dytor of Urban Catalyst, one of the country's most progressive and imaginative property developers. In due course, it was taken over by Employment Forum (UK). What follows is one of the reports of the construction training programme we ran with Alpha BSE.

STEP INTO CONSTRUCTION 2: Report of the Midtown
Foundation Multi-Skills Construction Training and Work
Experience Programme in Newham.
February to June 2004

INTRODUCTION

The Midtown Foundation, working with Alpha Building Services
& Engineering Ltd, has run a second multiskills construction
training and work experience programme, from February to June
2004. 20 people, mainly from black and minority ethnic groups
living in and around Newham, participated in the programme.
In addition, 10 more people received training in fork lift truck
driving and car valeting.

This follows an initial pilot multiskills construction training and
work experience programme run from September 2003 to late
January 2004 for 10 people, most of whom are now in full- or
part time employment.

This means that, between September 2003 and June 2004, 30
people will have benefited from the construction programme
– acquiring electrical, plumbing, plastering, painting and
decorating skills - and 10 from training in car valeting and fork
lift truck driving.

Training and work experience supervision has been provided
by Alpha, with Midtown taking responsibility for recruitment,
outreach and support, and accessing funds. Funding for the pilot
programme came from Jobcentre Plus, the Construction Industry
Training Board, Newham College of Further Education and the
London Borough of Newham, following an initial training grant
from GLE (Greater London Enterprise) through its Fast Forward
programme. For the second programme, funding was obtained
from Jobcentre Plus, CITB and the London Borough of Newham,
with training again provided by Alpha.

ACHIEVEMENTS

Results from the second programme have been encouraging. Most participants completed their training and work experience and over half have already found jobs or become self employed. The facilities of the Celestial Church in Manor Park have been significantly improved for wider community benefit. Shian Housing Association also provided work experience for four people, and there is a waiting list for future courses.

Stephen Timms, local MP and Minister of State in the DTI, presented certificates of achievement to the first 10 trainees and is the Guest of Honour at the presentation ceremony for participants in the second programme.

As with the pilot group of 10, many of those participating in the second programme were recruited through the Ethnic Minority Employment Outreach Programme being run by Employment Forum UK (Midtown's sister charity), at the Asian Friendship Centre in Katherine Road, Newham.

Employment Forum's outreach workers, Ilyas Ayoub, Madhu Samuels (herself a graduate of the first multiskills programme, and now working for Employment Forum), Shuma das Gupta and administration manager Jo Mackey provide advice and assistance to people coming to the centre on Mondays. Jobcentre Plus officials from the City & East London District Contact Team provide expert help in registering people for Jobseekers Allowance and searching for appropriate training and jobs. Advisers from Faith in London, the Muslim-led inter-faith regeneration company with whom we work closely (Faith in London is the lead partner for the Outreach Programme, which is funded by Jobcentre Plus) also play a vital role in advising clients and managing the programme.

As this programme has developed, our experience and expertise have grown and clients now receive a really helpful and much appreciated service – which has expanded from running on

Monday afternoons to running all day on Mondays.

Ilyas Ayoub, for the purposes of the construction project, is also employed part time by the Midtown Foundation and is responsible for supporting the trainees and assisting with jobsearch and many other matters.

Our relationship with Newham College has proved to be enormously helpful, and in particular with Alpha Building Services and Engineering Ltd. The multi-skills training provision and supervision of work experience have been crucial ingredients in the success of this programme, through which trainees, after 90 hours' training, gain a Newham College Access Diploma (NEWCAD). They also do a Health & Safety course (NVQ Level 2 Progression Award).

THE GROUP

The Newham residents participating in the second multiskills construction training and work experience programme have, in the main, proved to be able and keen to develop their knowledge and skills, as have those undertaking fork lift truck driving and car valeting training.

TRAINING CONTENT

In addition to the multi-skills construction course, trainees have also done an NVQ2 level (Progression Award) course in Health & Safety at Alpha BSE.

The group benefits from four special seminars: an evening session on jobsearch techniques and career development; a session learning how to access LearnDirect courses; an intensive training session with Jack Pinter of the National Theatre, doing communication and presentation skills; and an evening on starting, managing and running a business or becoming self employed.

Our intention throughout the programme has been to provide people not only with basic skills suitable for finding work in construction and other fields, but to equip them with skills that can be used at home and with 'different' skills and experiences which will enhance their opportunities to find good employment. In some cases, we expect people to seek further opportunities to train and achieve NVQ2 and beyond in whatever skills they wish to pursue...

NEXT STEPS

Recommendations from the pilot programme were as follows:

- ...in order to reach and work with people who are 'hard to reach', good support structures must be built into future programmes;
- ...that future programmes should offer 'sheltered' work experience and also work experience with the industry;
- ...where possible, such initial induction and training should be provided, in order to build confidence and trust among participants and familiarise them with a range of skills.

We have attempted to act on those recommendations and positive links have been established with four Housing Associations – Shian, who had four trainees on work experience and will take more trainees in future; East Thames Housing Group, who are keen to participate very actively in the programme and wish to involve their tenants; Genesis Housing Group, who, likewise, are interested in participating; and North London Muslim Housing Association, who have invited us to contact all their contractors with a view to providing work experience.

Our intention is to learn from the two programmes we have run and improve future programmes. Each multiskills construction training course will run for two days per week and, depending on the availability and needs of trainees, can be combined with English language and basic skills, IT and other training over a period of 3 months, followed by (or running concurrently with) work experience. Everyone will have the opportunity to participate in Health & Safety training and, we hope, in a First Aid course. Our aim is to create a system which can, over 12 months, enable up to 100 people to participate and benefit.

The training is now becoming properly integrated into Alpha's mainstream work, funded through Newham College of Further Education.. Jobcentre Plus have likewise played a crucial part in helping us to identify and recruit unemployed people onto the programme and in supporting them with travel and childcare costs. The involvement of the City & East London District Contact Team has enabled advice and guidance to be available during and outside normal working hours. This continues to be a positive and creative partnership and Jobcentre Plus has agreed to continue its involvement with future programmes.

We are now at the point of being able to employ people ourselves and an opportunity to work for a property developer on housing refurbishment has arisen. We commended one of the trainees (now working as self employed in construction) for a job locally, for which he quoted and was successful in obtaining. And we are in discussion with funders about expanding and enlarging the programme.

The Construction Industry Training Board, through its *Step into Construction* programme, has provided us with the funding needed to run good work experience programmes for both programmes held to date. Through their generous support we have been able to test the market, improve community facilities and give our trainees real opportunities to enhance and demonstrate their skills, under expert supervision and with the personal support we offer through our outreach workers. The benefits are there to be seen – people upskilled and into jobs and businesses...

As my work with Afghan Action developed, I had less involvement with Alpha BSE until John asked me to help with an industrial relations problem he was experiencing. He then asked me to do some more work to help promote Alpha BSE – it was, at that time, facing major issues as the economic downturn began to bite. In late 2008 I went in one day to find John in despair. He had taken the site over after it had stood derelict for 25 years and now paid a low rent for it. He had put in, over the previous five years, over £1 million in making the premises safe and bringing them back into use.

"Thames Water has put the site on the market without telling us, and we've got agents bringing prospective buyers around" he said. We decided at once to write to the Chief Executive of Thames Water, copying our letter to others in the company as well as local MPs Lyn Brown and Stephen Timms. Within 24 hours, we had a reply. The Chief Executive of Thames Water offered Alpha first refusal.

At the time, banks had virtually stopped lending and the prospects looked bleak – but within a month, John had obtained a loan from Lloyds TSB and was able to purchase the site.

I continued working with John and Alpha and, in July 2010, compered Alpha's Presentations Ceremony, to which an old friend, Nick McKemey, came. Nick was, at the time, Head of School Improvement at the Church of England's National Society in Church House, Westminster. He was very impressed at the high turnout of students who had come to receive their certificates – and deeply moved by their words of gratitude and determination. And it was he who mentioned a new kind of school being pioneered by a trust, formed by Kenneth Baker, former Secretary of State for Education, and Ron Dearing, former Head of the Post Office and Chair of the Working Party which, five years earlier, had conducted a major review of Anglican Schools and recommended that the Church of England expand its secondary provision and develop academies. The Baker Dearing Education Trust has been the prime mover behind the development of University Technical Colleges, and they are briefly described earlier in this chapter.

John Budu-Aggrey and his team have been passionate about providing the highest quality training in a wide range of construction-related skills. Alpha BSE is undoubtedly the most diverse construction training centre in London – probably in the country – and over 1000 students a year benefit from its courses. It provides training for adults wishing to acquire or improve their qualifications as well as over 140 apprenticeships and multi-skills courses for young unemployed men and women. It also provides courses for secondary school pupils from schools in nearby Waltham Forest.

At Easter 2013, we received the decision of the Department for Education – our application was successful and we should begin to work towards the London Design & Engineering UTC being ready to open in September 2015. The key partners, with Alpha, are the University of East London, Thames Water, Canary Wharf, Tribune Business Systems, Newham Council and the Diocese of Chelmsford.

One more thing.

In February 2013, Lord Andrew Adonis, Schools Minister in the Labour Government, wrote an article welcoming the new Archbishop of Canterbury, Justin Welby, and making the suggestion that there should be a Welby Commission on Apprenticeships and Youth Unemployment. In 2010, Our St Michael's Parochial Church Council had passed a motion, subsequently endorsed by the Deanery of Ampthill and described in a General Synod debate on Youth Unemployment in November 2012, that

"the Church of England should invite its dioceses, parishes and organisations to encourage those contracting to supply goods and services (eg in the field of construction and building maintenance) to employ one or more apprentices".

In a briefing paper I prepared for the Diocese of St Albans, I wrote:

> According to the Church Commissioners, "In 2006, necessary repairs to all listed places of worship in England were valued

at £925m over the next five years, or £185m a year. Around £110 million is currently spent on repairs to Church of England churches per annum, 70% of it raised by the congregations and local community".

We also know that there is a serious problem in the construction industry with an ageing workforce and, therefore, an urgent need to encourage young people into construction-related trades and, in particular, to grow a generation able to maintain, sustain and repair the wonderful heritage for which we, the C of E, are responsible.

So what can be done? We can follow the example of local authorities and others and include in our tendering processes a requirement that contractors employ apprentices. We can consult with Government, companies, trusts and others to set up a special mechanism for employing young people as apprentices and allocating them to help contractors and gain experience of work. We can find ways of "clustering" small companies and self employed builders so that no one company has to carry an unfair burden. We can seek financial and practical support from a myriad of organisations – including many people and congregations with a heart for our nation's youth.

What we cannot do is wring our hands and bemoan the fate of our young people – but carry on as though nothing can be done.

Young people aged 16 – 25 are precisely those least likely to belong to local Churches. We have the opportunity to create jobs and real hope – and this opportunity should grasped eagerly and positively.

With imagination and a genuine desire to serve God by helping young people, resources can be found to organise practical ways forward and enable a significant impact to be made. While the Church should not seek to use this approach as a means of proselytising, it should certainly use it as a new and exciting way to reach out to young people by responding to their need.

Training and employment offer young people the chance to acquire skills and discover their unique destiny. This will help them in the transition to adulthood and encourage them to take responsibility for their own lives. Without training, skills and employment, young people will become disillusioned and dependent. This is a stark denial of the Christian understanding of what it means to be human – and the Diocese should now explore what might be possible, drawing on the expertise and experience of people within the Diocese and beyond. (from a briefing paper produced for the St Albans Diocese, April 2012).

I wrote to Andrew Adonis with these ideas and got a positive response – endorsing them.

CHAPTER 10

CHRISTIAN NEWS – SIX ARTICLES

One of the things I really value is the discipline of penning a monthly article for *Christian News*. More often than not, I exceed my space limit and the long suffering Editor, Angela Price, has to trim the words. What a great job she does and how impressive the magazine is – certainly it must be among the best Church mags in the country. Its readership has grown steadily over recent years, to the point where plans are beginning to emerge to turn it into a social enterprise which can employ staff as well as make use of volunteers. The aim is to identify new markets in order to generate the income needed to sustain and expand the business.

My intention in selecting the articles which follow is to help generate funds needed to grow and develop the Churches' work in Woburn Sands. I've selected six articles from among those I've written over the past four years. Some are quite time specific. Some are focused on politics, others on the life of the Church and there are seasonal themes too. I'm always interested in context – and we Brits need constantly to remind ourselves that we're part of a wider world community. Just as those of us who belong to Churches need constantly to remind ourselves that we're not apart, we are part of society, and have much to offer and much to learn.

It's a bit of a surprise when I look back to my College days in Durham, in the mid 1970s, and remember that, in my three years of theological training, there was no study at all of any other faith than Christianity – and Old Testament Judaism. Islam, Hinduism, Sikhism, Buddhism and the myriad different faiths to be found not just across the world but in our own country just didn't feature. Maybe they were less prominent in those days in Britain, but what a huge gap in our education and preparation for ministry. And so it is in much of the British Church today. We seem not to notice the different faith communities around us, especially if they're not prominent in our particular community.

In my final year of training, my Pastoral Studies tutor asked me if I'd be interested in doing some work for a theologian in Teesside, Margaret Kane. She was writing a book and wanted someone to research – and write up – what Christians have said about 'work' over the years. That study was to change my life. I discovered the power and influence in world affairs of economic forces. Again a theme barely touched on in College, the world of work shapes people's lives, gives them identity and purpose, influences their ideas, their visions, their aspirations, their hopes, their fears...

JANUARY 2011

It's been a rough old winter! The worst weather on record, the coldest December, widespread snow causing travel and transport chaos... what a time we had of it.

Several times over the past few weeks I've moaned to myself "I'm dying.." – which, of course, in one sense I am, as we all are.. but really I'm not, I've just had a nasty dose of flu! More seriously, the terrible times people had at airports and railway stations in the great freeze before Christmas prompted comments such as "It's like living in a third world country" and "It's like being in a war zone". We know what was meant, but actually such sentiments – like my moaning – are good examples of bad language. Of course, Heathrow was nothing like a third world country, where life can seem so cheap and things are genuinely hard for many millions all the time – and it wasn't at all like a war zone, where terrified people don't know what to expect at any time and bombs, bullets and now drones are a constant source of terror.

Of course, there are so many causes for concern. Our country's finances are desperate and the real pain of the Government's policies to balance the books is going to hurt us all. And we have witnessed those devastating floods in Brazil, Australia and Sri Lanka, following last year's awful floods in Pakistan and Haiti's cataclysmic earthquake.

So here's a challenge for 2011. Beware of loose language. Let's use our language carefully. The old saying about sticks and stones ("can break your bones but words can never hurt you") is as wrong now as it ever was. Words can suggest and deceive, they can mock and lie, they can create the wrong impression and cause deep hurt.

The comments about being in a third world country or a war zone are interesting. It is because of poverty, natural disaster, oppression and war that millions of people leave their homes and move to wherever they can, seeking safety, security and sustenance. The statistics are terrifying, with nearly 4 million refugees in Asia and the Pacific alone. In the debates about immigration, refugees and overcrowding of our small island, our language can sometimes be imprecise and intemperate.

"Why should they invade our space? Why should they be allowed to benefit from our welfare system?" Legitimate questions? Well, maybe. But not dealt with by simplistic answers. Scratch the surface, and we discover that our forebears, the great British Empire builders of the 18th and 19th centuries, actually set us up for a whole host of problems. If you conquer another country, make its inhabitants your subjects (often second class subjects), gear up its agriculture and industry to meet your needs back home, don't be surprised by unintended consequences!

Rather like the Americans after the invasion of Iraq. Or the allies in their ongoing struggle to tame Afghanistan.

Words are the best we've got to describe what's going on in our lives. We use words to explain and interpret the world. Words serve to shape our values and views, they give life to our feelings and opinions, they are immensely powerful.. as the people of Jesus' day knew so well. After all, wasn't Jesus himself described, in the opening chapter of St John's Gospel, as "the Word made flesh"?

So now is a good time for reflection – and a bit more precision.

Christians and people of good will seek to nurture values of love, joy, peace, longsuffering, patience and so on – and impart them to our children and families. Those values can be seen in the life and example of Jesus. That's why it is interesting to reflect on how "the Word" is "made flesh" in our own lives and experiences.

Our Christian worldview is formed by the evidence of history and a heavy dose of realism. It is informed and challenged by the exercise of our consciences. It is supported by good and searching debate and questioning.

And the power of a book, the 400th anniversary of which we celebrate this year – the King James Bible. The Bible – in its older and more modern translations - teaches us that human beings, born in innocence, don't remain perfect. A deep vein of sin runs through us and permeates and pollutes the systems and structures we evolve to manage our lives and societies. History reinforces that view of the world.

I'm an optimist, but I recognise the deep flaws that run through our beautiful world. Take the pain of unemployment and poverty which are already beginning to make a deep impact on our own country. Look at the greed of the bankers and the weakness of Government to call them to account. Look at our governance – the expenses scandal has created the most onerous and crippling – graceless – system for monitoring expenses that it is in danger of leading to paralysis. And, more pertinently for so many people, look at the suffering of illness and injury, sometimes over many years. Hard to explain – hard to live with.

And yet, through these dark situations, so often the most amazing light shines.

Thank God!

So what can be done? What can we do?

1. Let's use our language carefully. The values we hold as Christians can seem so often to be contrary to much of the rest

of society. We value people whoever they are – and don't jump to conclusions about others. We believe in people – we hope against hope that God will do good in his world. So - challenge prejudice, question simplistic assumptions, speak out of turn..

2. Let's remind ourselves that Jesus' death – which came about as a direct result of the life he lived – was not the end. In fact, God's raising Jesus from the dead is his vindication of the life Jesus lived which led to the death he died..

3. Let's make our new year's resolution: what's good enough for him is good enough for us. Amidst all the doom and gloom, let's get out there with some good news – that God is at work in the world.. and we've signed up to help promote those visions and values which accord with God's way of doing things – rooted in love and open to all people.

FEBRUARY 2010

Not long now! There's nothing we can do to stop it. No more procrastination. No more pushing it to the back of our minds. It's unavoidable. And we're going to have to do something about it.

You've probably guessed what I'm talking about. The General Election, when we go to the polls to elect That Lot. Though this time round, there'll be a very different bunch to That Lot, and even those who stand again for election will be doing so much chastened, reminded that their high calling – and the calling to serve as a politician is a high calling – demands much and expects even more than sometimes might be humanly possible.

We've had a field day bashing politicians and now it's time to take the candidates seriously and examine their policies and programmes to see what they plan to offer. And to challenge them to spell out what they're promising and then hold them to it.

But how do we distinguish between them? The press and media

keep angling for differences and we now have several weeks and mountains of guff to go through before we get our chance to vote.

So here are a few pointers that help me in my own thinking and analysis about politics and much else. I derive them from various sources, including my growing understanding of my faith as revealed in the Scriptures, expounded and developed in the teachings and reflections of the Church and others, and tested in my conscience. These "pointers" (I can't really think of a better word) are set in the context of the wider knowledge and experience I've gleaned over many years, so, in practise, there's a kind of circular process going on – what a famous Latin American theologian has called a "hermeneutic circle". New issues and experiences challenge my views and understandings, which then challenge how I interpret the Bible and my Christian faith, which then inform how I respond to issues and learn from experience, which then get challenged by another new and unfamiliar situation.. and so on!.

Hermeneutics is a word to be conjured with! If it sounds obscure, it ain't! We all do hermeneutics all the time, without realising. It has to do with interpretation – how we interpret the world and what's happening around us. Which none of us do in an unbiased way, as it happens. We're all shaped and influenced by all kinds of things over a lifetime as our "values" – what we give value to – are formed and refined and adapted and developed. For Christians, our values are related to our beliefs, our sense of belonging and our experience. Believing, belonging, behaving.. another circular process.

Take an example which challenges my belief in a loving and caring Heavenly Father. The appalling earthquake in Haiti has shocked and saddened us all. Why has it happened? And why to such poor and marginalised people?

One answer comes from across the pond, where a well-known American televangelist and former US presidential candidate, Pat Robertson, has stated that it's a consequence of voodoo – the Haitians have been sinning all these years by selling their souls to the devil.

It's his hermeneutics which lead him to make such a statement. His understanding and interpretation of various passages in the Bible, taken with his background, culture, experience and personality, produce something which, in my opinion, is crude and cruel. I must confess that I don't have any easy answers to the hard question Why? But my faith and conscience compel me to respond, somehow, and to set that response in a wider understanding of God's call to work for a just and peaceful world. And if there's judgment to be made, it applies not only to the dreadful Haitian dictators and their henchmen but to America and the West who have tolerated such poverty and violence for decades and done nothing to alleviate or change it.

Take another example. Women priests and bishops. A subject which has deeply split the Church of England and the Anglican Communion and threatened our relations with Rome. For some people, their conscience – formed by their understanding of their faith and reading of the Scriptures, and no doubt influenced by their upbringing, education, experience, and personality – makes them unwilling to accept women as clergy or bishops. This has to do with "headship" (a man should be head of the family), or the fact that Jesus' closest followers, the 12 disciples, were all men, or the long tradition in the Church of male clergy. Others interpret the Scriptures and teachings of the Church quite differently and believe that women are just as able as men to function as clergy or bishops and should be encouraged and enabled to do so.

And here's our old friend Hermeneutics again – urging us to understand and interpret the Bible in the light of our modern, contemporary experience. "You can't just take the words of the Bible literally", says Herman, "without exploring how they were understood and interpreted in their own situation and setting and then trying, imaginatively, to apply the underlying meaning in a quite different culture and situation today".

So let's take an example which applies to the murky world of politics and Government. In the New Testament, there are some interesting passages which need unpacking. Romans Chapter 13 is the clearest example of teaching about how to live and behave in relation to the Government. St Paul is quite clear – the State authorities are God given, he asserts, and should be respected. And if you misbehave, you deserve to be punished. He even says that "the man in authority" is "God's servant working for your own good".

There have in history been some pretty cruel rulers, and the Romans, in whose Empire Paul spent his whole life, were a pretty rotten bunch. If we think our politicians are bad, we should just have a look round the world today and then study a bit of history – and we'll see how truly ghastly most governments and rulers are and have been down the ages. But here comes Herman to the rescue.

Read Romans a bit more closely, he says. Take out the chapters and verses – they're a later invention and Paul didn't even use punctuation, let alone chapters, in his letters. Now read, say, from the start of the previous chapter, Chapter 12. It's all about offering yourselves as a living sacrifice, about not conforming to the world's standards but being transformed – from the inside. Be humble. Be convivial. Be generous with the gifts God has given you. Bless – yes, bless - your persecutors and repay people who hurt you with kindness. This is radical, earth shattering stuff – completely at variance with the way most people think or the Roman State operates. And don't (now we're moving into Chapter 13) make a big fuss about the State and how unfair That Lot are – just get on with living the transformative life of Christ. And that will challenge the State to its very core.

Martin Luther King and the Civil Rights Movement demonstrated the power of such an approach through their non-violent resistance to the oppressive racism of the States of Alabama, Georgia, Mississippi and the rest.

So what about the General Election? Now it's time for some real people power. We expect much of our elected representatives. Yes, much. And now we'll call them to account. We shouldn't expect the impossible. Nor should they try and legislate for every situation, because they can't. We need just laws which help us behave better, not poorly formulated and inadequately scrutinised laws which people ignore or find ways around.

Government's calling, in my view, is this: to promote the Common Good; to prevent wrongdoing; and to protect the poor and weak. I derive those principles from my Christian understanding and believe that all legislation should be tested against them. Of course there will be much debate and disagreement about how to achieve these core principles – but that's what I expect of my political leaders. That's what they're called to implement. And that's why they need our support and prayers.

APRIL 2011

"A first wave of around 600 Anglicans are officially leaving the Church of England in protest at the decision to ordain women as bishops. They will be enrolled as candidates to join a new branch of the Catholic Church - the Ordinariate - which has been specially created for them. They will attend Catholic Mass marking Ash Wednesday before spending Lent preparing to convert [just before Easter].

'We couldn't continue to be Christians in a normal sense when we were in a maverick Church that kept changing the rules to appease the common culture,' said Father Ed Tomlinson, a Tunbridge Wells priest and one of those leaving the Church of England.

He said changes to the rules on divorce and family had produced a 'political Church where people campaign for things'." (BBC News, 9 March 2011).

I can't go along with Fr Ed's 'maverick Church' analysis. The idea that the Gospel is so rooted in the past that there can be no adaptation to current situations is not how I understand the presence and activity of God at work in the world today. Looking back through history, we can see rather a lot of unsavoury things which the Church has too easily gone along with – burning people at the stake who disagree with the powers that be, for example... how could Christians ever, under any circumstances, support such behaviour? So how far back do we go before we get to the 'pure Church'?

The problem with the Fr Ed position is that it does rather pick and choose what it wants to assert as fundamental to faith. Ordaining women as priests or bishops is a problem for some people because Jesus' apostles were all male. But they were also all Jewish... The early Church at first thought only Jews could be followers of Jesus, the Jewish Messiah, and the book of Acts (author, St Luke, the writer of the 3rd Gospel) shows how, progressively, the Gospel became accessible to non Jewish people, the Gentiles. St Peter and St Paul, the two giants of the early Church, agreed that the Gospel was equally for the Gentiles but, in practise, poor old Peter struggled with the idea for a long time. In Paul's letter to the Christians of Galatia, he describes how he rounded on Peter and didn't half tell him off!

"..when Cephas [Peter] came to Antioch, I opposed him to his face, because he was clearly in the wrong. For until some messengers came from James [Jesus' brother and head of the mother Church in Jerusalem], he was taking his meals with Gentile Christians; but after they came, he drew back and began to hold aloof, because he was afraid of the Jews..." (Galatians 2, verses 11ff).

Galatians is one of my favourite letters. Paul is so passionate and so utterly committed to spreading the Good News of Jesus Christ to everyone, Jew, Gentile, male, female, slave, free... And can't you just hear the Peter group muttering away about maverick Paul, changing rules - and not just pandering to the culture but deliberately going way beyond current ideas and practises.

In a nutshell, I think the Ordinariate – and the idea of

'converting' from one Christian Church to another – is pandering to the past.

Much better would be an Extra-Ordinariate for people who think denominations are outmoded and increasingly irrelevant and want to be part of the Anglican Church, the Methodist Church, the Catholic Church – the One Church, the Body of Christ, the People of God.

How sad that we are not supposed to partake of the bread and wine, the Body and Blood of our Lord, in different churches. How sad that some denominations are so arrogant that they won't recognise the vocation to ordained ministry of other denominations.

A cursory read though St Matthew's Gospel would show quite clearly what Jesus thought of those Pharisees for whom Law was more important than grace, rules and regulations than love and faith.

Not all the Pharisees were baddies. But it was the Pharasaic party in the mother Church in Jerusalem who couldn't quite give up their old habits. When Paul and Barnabas reported on the amazing things happening among the Gentiles, the Pharasaic party insisted that Gentile converts should at least keep up appearances – "Those Gentiles should be circumcised and told to keep the Law of Moses" (Acts 15, verse 5).

I'm sure James must have been an Anglican. He found a good compromise between the Pharisaic party and Paul: "in my judgement.. we should impose no irksome restrictions on those of the Gentiles who are turning to God; instead we should instruct them by letter to abstain from things polluted by contact with idols, from fornication, from anything that has been strangled, and from blood..." (verses 19 – 21).

I'm not saying that Scripture or tradition don't matter. Far from it. I believe that we should be rooted in the past – deeply rooted so as to grow and develop. We should be living in the present –

which inevitably means being part of contemporary culture but in a constructively critical relationship with it. And looking to the future – working with one another, inspired by God's Holy Spirit to build a world in which all people, whoever they are and whatever their gender, can discover their worth and their true calling.

It is interesting to note that James and the Jerusalem Church listened carefully to Paul and Barnabas' report. They could see God was at work. And they were truly thrilled that Gentiles were responding so keenly to the Good News. It may have contradicted some deeply held views – and I dare say there was a minority who thought this was a compromise too far – but they affirmed what was happening.

Those joining the Ordinariate – and all of us – should be asking: what need we do to share the Good News in ways to which our contemporaries can respond?

Let's be extra-ordinary! Let's create an Extra-Ordinariate which truly cares about God's world (yes, today's world) and makes the pain of poverty, hunger, loneliness, disease and despair, war and conflict, environmental pollution, unemployment – all spiritual issues as much as physical – our priorities...

And, by the way, we have some truly wonderful women priests and ministers – and I'm sure James and the Jerusalem Church would look at the evidence and affirm their ministry without hesitation!

SEPTEMBER 2010

We'd just finished morning prayer one Friday in August when a thin man with a large rucksack came into church. He came over and asked: "Are you real Christians?". He had a heavy accent and explained that he was from Romania and had come to the UK looking for work as a chef – only to discover that he can't work here without a visa, which could take 6 months to obtain. Romania is a latecomer to the European Union and Romanians don't have the opportunities other EU citizens enjoy.

As we talked, we discovered Ovidiu was an interesting person with a deep faith and commitment. A chequered past had led him to hit rock bottom in a country with a desperate history under an authoritarian dictator (remember the dreadful Nicolai Ceaucescu and his ghastly wife Elena?) and, since the collapse of communism, two decades of poverty and struggle. Somewhere along the line, the friendship and support over a number of years of a local Christian pastor had made an impact on this man and he had discovered a deep and life-changing faith.

He'd come to Western Europe to make something of his life. And here he was, in St Michael's Church, looking for help as he made his way to Denmark, where Romanians can work without restrictions.

This was his story. And we had no way of telling whether it was true – except that he seemed a genuine person.

He gave me the email address of his pastor back home, so I sent a message and was delighted to hear back within 24 hours, complete with photos of the local church. The pastor vouched for Ovidiu and I wrote back saying thanks.

A few hours later, another email arrived from the pastor. Ovidiu had arrived in Lille. I got onto the internet and checked out the Anglican Chaplaincy in Lille – only to find that the lay reader was a long lost friend from university, whom I hadn't seen for 40 years. I phoned him and linked them up.

That's one of the benefits of being part of a worldwide community of fellow-travellers, people who aren't afraid to take the risk of putting themselves out. People who believe there really is hope for the world – if we just try to treat one another as human beings (what Jesus meant by "loving your neighbour", I suppose).

The same day, another email arrived – from a friend in Afghanistan.

"I am writing this email in complete shock. My friend's family home was raided last night by soldiers in the middle of the night in Kabul. They broke down the door and held guns to even the little children in their house. They hooded the three men in the house, my friend's 70 year old father, brother and cousin and even tried to handcuff and hood his little 9 year old son. There was no explanation, they were just taken away under anti-terrorism, which is complete madness. My friend's family have sacrificed many members of their family's lives to fight against the Taliban and other extremist groups. They have given their support to Western troops from the beginning and continue to support the Western intervention. It is absolute madness to raid the home of their own supporters. My friend's sister was even commended by Barak Obama for her work..".

These two unrelated stories raise for me two vital questions: what's this got to do with us? And what exactly is Britain's place in the world? Neither Romania nor Afghanistan – unlike many other countries across Africa, Asia and North America – were ever conquered by the British. And yet we have an affinity with both nations in different ways: Romania is a European country and part of the EU. Afghanistan is a country where we have made a huge commitment in the struggle for peace and justice. Both those countries are poor – desperately so.

The people of both have suffered hugely at the hands of monsters.

Whether we like it or not – and many people don't – both these countries are a part of us and our future is tied up with theirs. Failure in Afghanistan will mean the world is yet more dangerous and insecure. Poverty and unemployment in Romania makes for hordes of people seeking work in the West and sometimes turning up destitute on our doorsteps.

I could be writing about many other countries – not least Pakistan, where the devastating floods have caused unbelievable suffering and hardship. Or Haiti, still deeply traumatised and impoverished by the earthquake earlier in the year.

So when we're tempted to moan about a bus that doesn't turn up or a train that's late or slow traffic on busy roads or the lengthy queue in the local shop, remember plucky Ovidiu and those brave, beleaguered Afghans - and the people of northern Pakistan and Haiti, and the countless others around the world who can't be sure they'll even see another day.

I thank God for Britain. We are a nation with long and deep international experience and a truly global perspective. Our language is spoken more widely than any other on earth. Our influence remains pervasive and much appreciated. Our education and health services are much maligned but truly superb compared to most of the rest of the world. And people want to come here from all over the world because they know we are a just, functioning democratic nation – albeit imperfect, but still pretty good.

I believe we have a role to play in nudging the world towards justice, peace and respect for others. It takes courage – the courage to ignore the grumblers and moaners, the people who think that national self-interest is an exclusive, excluding thing which shuts its ears to the cries of pain in Romania, Afghanistan and elsewhere. Yes, we have problems at home – and these must – and can – be addressed. But we're part of a bigger world, a world where all have a place and deserve a future.

That is at the heart of what being a Christian is about. That's the real significance of our Christian heritage. Whether it's at local level or in the international arena, there is no time for complacency and certainly no time for sitting around complaining that the country's gone to the dogs. Jesus' conclusion, when he'd stunned his listeners with the story of the Good Samaritan, was brief and to the point: "Go thou and do likewise".

What a challenge! A challenge to make the world a place of

justice, peace and security – not just for us and our children, but for everyone.

And Ovidiu? He set off from Lille by coach to Denmark via Germany and we got a call from him en route. He should be there now – hopefully settling in well with a supportive group of friends at the Romanian Baptist Church in Copenhagen and a chance to earn a living.

OCTOBER 2012

In late September of this year, The House of Commons Environmental Audit Committee issued a serious warning. The melting of sea ice is now happening so fast the Arctic could be ice free in summer in the next few years... and that will have a direct impact on the UK's weather pattern, with such a huge amount of fresh, cold water melting into the sea.

"There is evidence that the melting Arctic may be affecting the gulf stream currents that bring warmth to the UK and Northern Europe and so may be behind the unusually cold winters that have been hitting the UK over the last few years," said Committee Chair Joan Whalley MP.

She pointed out that even when a run of dry winters is followed by a wet summer, as has happened this year in the UK, it will not make up for the risk of droughts.

"It is quite simple - the replenishment of aquifers generally occurs through the winter and into spring," she explained. "Once you get beyond April/ May time, the summer temperatures are high enough that even if we have a wet summer, it doesn't replenish the aquifers, a lot of the water evaporates away. We are concerned that if we continue to have a sequence of cold winters, that could be much more damaging, even with wet summers alongside them."

Water is a serious issue. And if we think we've got problems, just think how water – or lack of water – impacts in other parts of the world.

Internationally, 780 million people lack access to safe drinking water, according to the United Nations. By 2030, 47 per cent of the world's population will be living in areas of high water stress, according to the *Environmental Outlook to 2030* report of the Organisation for Economic Co-operation and Development.

Of all the water on earth, only 3% is fresh, with less than 1% of drinkable water easily accessible. And don't be surprised to find that, where access to clean water is a problem, there is already serious political conflict – in Afghanistan in 2010, for example, 92% of the million population did not have access to proper sanitation, making it top of the list of "the worst places in the world for sanitation" (according to USAID). 25% of children under 5 are affected every year by diseases originating from poor and/or bad sanitation.

I would observe that, after over a decade of huge international intervention in Afghanistan and billions of dollars invested to create a safe and viable country, there is still widespread drought and severely limited access to clean water.

Jesus knew the importance of water, coming from a hot and dusty land. Water featured frequently in his stories and teaching, drawing, as he did so often, on the many powerful references in the Old Testament to God as the "spring of living water" (according to the prophet Jeremiah) or the source of thirst-quenching refreshment and succour - "As the deer pants for streams of water, so my soul pants for you, O God. My soul thirsts for God, for the living God" (Psalm 42).

But Jesus goes further. At the great Jewish Festival of Tabernacles in Jerusalem, each day there was a procession of priests to the pool of Siloam to draw water and bring it back to the Temple to pour out as a libation at the morning sacrifice. On the last day, with the Festival at its climax, Jesus dramatically cries out loudly,

"If anyone is thirsty, let him come to me and drink" (John 7, v37).

This audacious, outlandish claim will cost him his life. A life given not just as an example of what good people can be like, nor even just to bring faith to those individuals who hear his message and want to do something in response. This is a life given to bring real nurture, true refreshment, to the whole world.

So the future use of water and fair access for all people everywhere is of direct relevance to God's plan for his world - and Jesus' act of self-giving, sacrificial love.

Oh, by the way. In St Michael's Church, it's the Sunday School youngsters who have realised the importance of water before the rest of us – and raised money for Water Aid. Thank you for your example – the rest of us should follow your lead.

DECEMBER 2009

Have you heard the awful news? A transport strike could be on the cards for Christmas.

Everyone's up in arms complaining.. But what's to be done? The Transport and General Reindeers Union are a prickly bunch and poor Santa and his senior management team are locked in negotiations with Dasher, Dancer, Blixen and radical activist Rudolph the Red. It's all to do with flying hours and tachometers and health and safety and so on. And pay of course.

"We're a bit upset about pension arrangements" Rudolph told *Christian News* in an exclusive interview last week. "Not only is the pot dry, but there seems to be no prospect of ever being able to retire - and the delivery list gets no shorter".

There's even talk of referring Santa to the Monopolies Commission and privatising the service, but that's gone down like a lead balloon with customers.

Joking aside, we live in a complex and changing world! Old traditions and ways of doing things are under constant scrutiny and new practises are often ill conceived and ineffective. Things like 'political correctness' and 'health and safety' are increasingly derided as impositions, stifling our creativity and enjoyment. Actually, they originate from good motives, their intention being to improve the lives of everyone, especially people with particular needs.

Think, for example, of the treatment of British orphans only 60 years ago, sent off to a new life in Australia or Canada where, they were told, they would be welcomed and loved. At least we are more aware now of the effects of such actions, not necessarily intended to be malicious by the authorities, but, as we now know, cruel and ill-conceived, with devastating consequences for some.

Or consider the language about – and treatment of – people with learning difficulties and disabilities. Four decades ago, I worked in a unit for autistic children linked to a large hospital for 'subnormals', as people there were called. I remember only too well the elderly adults who came from the hospital to tend our unit's gardens. One of them had lived at that hospital all his life – placed there for being deaf and from a family to poor to cope.

Our sins may be more sophisticated now, but they're still as sinful! Wealthy bankers, having been bailed out by us taxpayers, still think they're entitled to big bonuses. In fact, it seems to be the case that to get the 'best' people you have to pay large salaries, while the rest of us are motivated by a sense of duty! The scandal of what are perceived to be greedy people in the public sector is just as galling, whether BBC or local government executives or some of our members of Parliament.

And in case we think it's just 'them' that contravene the laws of common decency, I don't think any of us can honestly say that we have never misbehaved or tried it on! St Paul put it more bluntly in his letter to the Romans: "for all have sinned and fallen short of the glory of God".

If ever the 'glory of God' was compromised, it was at Christmas. A defenceless, dependent baby born into a dangerous and unpredictable world.

We speak of the Mystery of the Incarnation in our Carol Services - and, for me, that phrase conjures up flickering candles and carols and a sense of warmth and familiarity.

Actually, the Mystery of the Incarnation was a pretty squalid affair. Giving birth in a stable, with scruffy shepherds piling in to see what's going on and vicious soldiers scouring the Bethlehem streets slaughtering infants. This baby was soon to be whisked off as a refugee to the safety of Egypt. He may even have spent his early years in a refugee camp.

One of the great things about Christmas-time is the chance it can give us to pause and take stock. It's a time for reflection and we should try and use it to put things into perspective – the perspective of an infant born in poverty to young, inexperienced parents alone in a strange place, that stable probably a cave behind a pub in a noisy street, surrounded by animals and flies..

Infants are totally dependent for their very survival on those who care for them – and Jesus was no different. Almighty God may be his father, but at that time, in that place, Jesus was no different to countless billions of human beings who have, each one, started life like that.

Such thoughts put our current preoccupations into a different perspective.

Thank God for Christmas – but don't let's stop there.. Let's pick up the challenge of the Incarnation, to build a new world to echo the angels' song of praise: "Glory to God in the highest and on earth peace and goodwill to all…".

This Christmas, let's go for glory!

CHAPTER 11

SERMONS AND ADDRESSES

I have chosen a small selection of sermons and addresses I've given in St Michael's and elsewhere over the past few years. It is my practise to write sermons out in full, though I don't read them when delivering them. The discipline of writing them helps me to think through what I'm trying to say and having the written text there serves both as a prompt and a source of reassurance.

I have selected five sermons, two preached at churches in South East London and three from my time in Woburn Sands. I suppose the real test will be whether any of the St Michael's congregation can actually remember any of those three St Michael's sermons. I don't think I'll ask!

BAPTISM OF JOBIE DAVIES: THE CHURCH OF THE GOOD SHEPHERD, LEE, SOUTH EAST LONDON.
Sunday 13 August 2000: Texts - Ephesians 4, 25 to 5, 2. John 6, 35, 41 – 51

INTRODUCTION

Here's a poser for people of about my age (25) and older…

Can you name 3 Westerns you used to watch on black-and-white television… The Lone Ranger; Laramie; Bonanza etc

We didn't get our own telly till I was 11! Can you imagine that? Life without TV. I was an avid fan of cowboys and indians. I used to listen to Matt Dillon on Wednesday nights at some unearthly hour (8 o'clock), and on Saturdays we were allowed to go to Mr and Mrs Hunter's down the road, to watch Laramie on their television.

TOY STORY 2

Next question: can you name a very popular film which came out only a year or so ago, and has in it.. a cowboy, a cowgirl, a prospector and a horse called Bullseye?

Toy Story 2. A brilliant cartoon, which I strongly recommend to anyone who hasn't seen it...

I don't want to spoil the plot (sorry, I'm going to anyway), but in the story, Woody the cowboy toy meets up with his cowgirl companion Jessie, his old horse Bullseye and an old prospector puppet.. and discovers that he, Woody, was once the star of a 1950s children's TV series.

The old series is replayed, and Woody, the hero, in the last episode has seconds to save the others from certain disaster as the mine explodes and … and… the programme never got completed, and the space age arrived, and cowboys became yesterday's toys, and…

LOOSE ENDS

There are lots of loose ends in our lives, aren't there. Lots of things which don't get completed, words left unsaid, deeds left undone, relationships unfulfilled and friendships allowed to wither.. if only.. if only..

PRINCE OF EGYPT

Another popular cartoon, this time from the Disney stable, came out a couple of years ago, called *The Prince of Egypt.* It's all about a character called Moses, who grows up in the luxury of the King of Egypt's court. Not until he's a grown up does he realise that he was an adopted child, discovered in a floating basket on the river by Pharoah's daughter when he was just a baby..

Really he was a child of the Israelites, the slaves treated like dirt by the cruel Pharoah and his soldiers.

If you want to read the full, unabridged version of the story – The Great Escape is an apt title for it – have a look in the Book of Exodus, in your Bibles.

That Great Escape is a fascinating story spanning many years, a story still remembered every Friday evening by Jewish people as they recall the basis for their historic faith – out of which our own Christian faith has grown. Far from thinking that politics and religion don't mix, that Great Escape, the Exodus from Egypt, is based on direct confrontation with power, injustice and exploitation. Moses, the playboy prince, became the leader of the revolution, the one who finally had the guts to stand before Pharoah and tell him - "Enough is enough. Your slaves are leaving Egypt for freedom.. and we're leaving now".

Talking of loose ends, even Moses dies with his great dream unfulfilled – he never makes it to the Promised Land himself…

JESUS – BORN UNDER ROMAN OCCUPATION

When Jesus is born in Bethlehem, the City of David, Israel's greatest king, he is born in the Promised Land, but much of the promise has been dissipated. The nation is enslaved not to Egypt now, but to Rome. And Jesus lives his entire life in enemy occupied territory. The Jewish nation may have longed for freedom, but Rome rules, and rules with a firm hand. No wonder they start to pay attention to the young populist from up north, stirring the crowds up with dangerous ideas, rocking the boat and upsetting even the leaders of his own people. Jesus offers a new kind of hope… his teaching, his healing, his love for the sinners and outcasts, his conviction that everyone counts, everyone matters, everyone belongs… this quickly threatens the public order, the uneasy peace which Jewish leaders and Roman Governor strive to maintain..

But this man Jesus goes further when he makes outlandish and blasphemous claims about his own relationship with God the Creator – which could have been ignored if he's proved to be just another eccentric or madman… but the problem is, he is so transparently good.. generous, open, warm, courageous, challenging… the nearest anyone has ever seen to a 'complete' person..

From the point of view of the Roman Governor and the puppet King of Palestine, the execution of one more rabblerouser is neither here nor there, all in a day's work.

But for Jesus and his followers, the end has come too soon, the work is incomplete, the business unfinished… more loose ends…

Well.. no, actually, that's not the way it is!

THE CROSS

As Jesus hangs on the cross, what appears to be the lowest point in the history of the universe, the defeat of goodness and the destruction of any hope for change – is transformed by a great, agonising cry - "It is finished".. my life's work is completed.. the work Jesus set out to do, to live for others as a "model" for humanity, has been achieved..

Of course it's upset the powerful.. of course it's been offensive to those who think they know best.. of course it threatens the very foundations of civilised society.. how can the world possibly carry on if people stop respecting their leaders and just get on with living openly and generously?

BAPTISM

What's all this got to do with Baptism?

Well poor old Jobie here is identifying himself with the cause of that one who died a shameful, criminal death on the cross. Jobie is saying – I want to be part of that movement for change, I want to help build a new world, I believe in love and justice, I am opposed to selfishness, greed and jealousy.

And I say "poor old Jobie" because the poor little fellow hasn't got a clue about all this! He can't consent because he can't even speak, let alone understand!

THREE KEY ELEMENTS

That's why we need three key elements:

• parents and family.. the ones who help him live the dangerous life of Jesus and sustain him in doing so..
• godparents.. the ones who pray for him and support and encourage him and his family in practical and spiritual ways..
• and the Church, the followers of Jesus who have already made that commitment for themselves, and understand the danger of working for a just and loving community and world… and so will do all they can to stand alongside Jobie..

The baptism of a small child is like acting out a play of something before it's happened. In baptism, Jobie's whole life flashes before him, all those loose ends, all that unfinished business, all those things he'll wish he'd done or not done, said or not said.. in his baptism his name, Jobie Llewellyn Davies, is forever identified with that of Jesus Christ.

.. and that means dying to the old ways of doing things, living selfishly as though no one else matters but himself.. and rising to new life with Christ, a life given for others, a life committed to building that new world where everyone matters, everyone has a chance, everyone is a child of God, and therefore worthy of the highest respect and greatest love.

CHURCH OF THE CROSS, THAMESMEAD, SOUTH EAST LONDON

Sunday 13 October 2002: Text - Philippians 4, verses 1 - 9

Has anyone seen the latest film by Ken Loach, the Director of *Kes*? It's called *Sweet Sixteen* and is rated 18 – even though it's about 15 - 16 year old boys in a depressed seaside town in Scotland. We went to see it last week – and I have to tell you that I was already scared witless by the trailers for the forthcoming 18 programmes.. so when the film started, I wasn't sure what to expect.

Surprisingly, it's a film with no sex, less violence than East Enders and an almost unintelligible Scottish dialect (it has sub-titles for the first 15 minutes of the film). So why is it rated 18? Because the characters in the film speak in exactly the way youngsters speak to each other in deeply deprived urban areas. Lots of bad language. Lots of foul language. In some ways, there are similarities between where the film is set and parts of South London, including Thamesmead. Kids who have dropped out of school and have no hope of getting qualifications. Broken families and parents overwhelmed – a prison visit to see the mother of the film's teenage hero is how it starts. Then there's the drugs… their widespread use and their terrible effects. And the local mafia and their power and influence.

WHAT YOU SOW, YOU REAP

The film's message is deeply depressing. What you sow, you reap.

My father was a schoolmaster of the old fashioned sort. And he would often quote the Authorised Version of Galatians 6 verse 7:

"Be not deceived; God is not mocked: for whatsoever a man soweth, that also shall he reap. For he that soweth unto his own flesh shall of the flesh reap corruption; but he that soweth unto the Spirit shall of the Spirit reap eternal life. And let us not be weary of welldoing: for in due season we shall reap, if we faint not".

What you sow, you reap.

That's not to say that the characters in the film are all bad and deserve what they get. I know it's becoming unfashionable now to pity the perpetrators of crime, but you can't help feeling sad at the mess these kids and adults are in and angry at the way they've been left to rot on the margins of society. The sowing and reaping applies to individuals and families. It also applies to society and nation – and that means we all share some of the responsibility.

I went to see my MP last week to press him to oppose unilateral invasion of Iraq. And in the waiting room with me was someone from a local housing estate, there to complain about the drug dealing in a house down the road – and the unwillingness of the police to do anything, even though it was so blatant.

People feel powerless. Even good people try and try.. and give up

TOO INWARD LOOKING

In the churches, we're prone to spend far more time and effort on internal matters than we should. And we can sometimes be trapped by the institutional pressures.. when on our doorstep there's a world of Sweet Sixteens desperate for our involvement, love and service.

"The Lord is near", St Paul says in today's epistle (Philippians 4 vv5ff);

"..do not be anxious, but in everything make your requests known to God in prayer and petition with thanksgiving. The peace of God, which is beyond understanding, will guard your hearts and your thoughts in Jesus Christ. And now, my friends, all that is true, all that is noble, all that is just and pure, all that is loveable and attractive, whatever is excellent and admirable – fill your thoughts with these things. Put into practise the lessons I taught you, the tradition I passed on, all that you heard me say or saw me do; and the God of peace will be with you".

We're into sowing and reaping again, aren't we?

AGONY AUNT PAUL

Now this is practical advice. If you read the newspapers or weeklies, you'll find advice pages, won't you, with practical tips from Agony Aunts about what to do. There's everything from advice about getting stains out of the tablecloth to illnesses and allergies to problems with the kids and relationships of all sorts.

So here's Aunty Paul writing his advice column in the *Philippi Standard…* and he says:

"The Lord is near". That could mean the End of the World is nigh.. or it could just mean God is close to us, among us, within us, so.. "don't be anxious". Worry breeds worry. Think of those poor people in Washington at present, with a lone lunatic sniping and killing random individuals at petrol stations and on the streets. Everyone is nervous about going out and doing all the normal things life requires – walking to school, shopping, filling up with petrol, visiting friends.. Or think how nervous parents are about letting their kids play out – always having to keep a close eye and constant check, for fear of them being kidnapped or harmed.

Of course, we know statistically that there is only the tiniest chance of any of us being endangered like that.. but nevertheless..

CONVERSATIONAL PRAYING

"Don't be anxious, but in everything make your requests known to God in prayer and petition with thanksgiving". When we plead with God and open up our hearts to him in desperation, he understands, he knows what we're feeling. Prayer can be hard work, can't it? So often, our minds wander when we try to concentrate on praying, and we don't get all the praying done that we should.

Think of prayer as a conversation with God. When we're chatting after this service at coffee, the conversations will go all over the place. We may start by asking someone how they are and end up hearing about their holiday in China and what the Great Wall is like! That could lead into a conversation about history and archaeology and someone's school coursework, and then into the A level fiasco and then onto qualifications and jobs..

If God created us with such creative potential, we should expect conversations with Him to be discursive too!

Paul talks about the "peace of God, which is beyond all understanding" guarding our "hearts and thoughts". So, if the Spirit of God dwells within us, we can expect his inspiration when we pray or think or agonise or weep or laugh.

Do a little test when you next have some time to stop and think.

Offer your time to God.. and see what happens. Your thoughts and ideas will, after not very long, find their way to something important .. something that matters to you.. something which you can do something about. Prayer and action are always connected. That's why praying is dangerous! But also, it brings peace – because when we commit to doing what we should be doing with our lives or our time or our skills or our energy or our love, however tough it is, we can be mentally and spiritually at peace because we're doing the right thing.

Paul goes on to say: "fill your thoughts" with all that is true, noble, just, pure, loveable, attractive, excellent and admirable.

This is about sowing.. because what you sow, you reap.

PROGRAMMING

Paul's actually talking about programming.

I'm not much cop with computers. And I could certainly never be a computer programmer. I am amazed at the ability of computers - and even more amazed at the ability of the programmers who have created the computer programmes. Good programmers have to have logical minds. Because these machines are not humans, they're machines, conditioned to work in logical ways, step by step (step by very very quick step!). Now, when I turn my computer on, it sometimes doesn't work as it should. Or I press the wrong keys. And I feel sometimes like picking it up and chucking it through the window. What I really need is training, discipline, patience and practise.

"Put into practise", Paul says, "the lessons I taught you, the tradition I passed on, all that you heard me say or saw me do; and the God of peace will be with you".

What you sow, you reap. And, if you remember the Parable of the Sower, "some seed fell into good soil, where it came up and grew, and produced a crop; and the yield was thirtyfold, sixtyfold, even a hundredfold" (Mark 4 v8).

You live the life of Christ – and leave God to do the rest.

PATRONAL FESTIVAL AND BACK TO CHURCH SUNDAY. ST MICHAEL'S CHURCH, WOBURN SANDS.
Sunday 27 September 2009: Text - Matthew 14, 22 - 33

I'd like to introduce you to three friends. They're here today and you may well be sitting next to them.

The first one is a bit of a dreamer. He's an eternal optimist but never really believes that what he hopes for is going to happen. If only.. if only.. That's his name, by the way. If only I could win the lottery, I could pay off the mortgage and help the kids out and..

If only.. I was at a conference recently and heard about a charity called the Jet Foundation which had invested $100 million with the American financier Bernard Madoff and was going to give $400,000 to the work of Clive Stafford-Smith, the British lawyer who helps innocent people on death row in America, and helps people imprisoned in Guantanamo Bay. If only they hadn't put so many eggs into one basket! Terribly important work has now lost out on a major donation of $400,000 because Madoff has turned out to be fraudulent.

My second friend is quite a sceptic. He should have been a financial adviser to the Jet Foundation! He's called Ah but.. You have a great idea, you're buzzing with excitement - and his automatic response is: Ah but.. Ah but, have you ever thought about how difficult it is to get people off death row. Anyway, we tried it before and it didn't work. Ah but is a true Englishman – his first reaction is caution!

Then there's my third friend, young, giggly and rather gullible. Very likeable, always enthusiastic. Whatever you say is met with this response: Oh wow.. Clive Stafford-Smith's work is pretty amazing. He helps innocent people unjustly imprisoned.. Oh wow..

If only, Ah but, Oh wow.. all genuine, all distinctive, and all three sat here today among us, in various combinations!

One day, If only, Ah but and Oh wow were in a boat together. I'll explain why in a moment.

They were friends and followers of a remarkable young man called Jesus. A man who was the talking point in every shop and on every street corner around the towns and villages of Galilee.

A man with a reputation.. so much so that, despite the fact that the climate is baking hot and it's sticky and dusty and the roads are pretty rough - and air conditioned transport isn't going to be invented for another 2000 years - word has got round and huge numbers of people have been turning out to see him and hear him and, in some cases, even be healed by him of their illnesses and afflictions.

It's actually been quite tough lately for Jesus. He went home the other day – back to Nazareth where he grew up. He went and spoke in the local church – called a synagogue in those days – and, unlike everywhere else, where people were thrilled and excited by him, here the place was full of Ah buts.

"Where does he get this wisdom from and these miraculous powers? Is he not the carpenter's son? Isn't his mother called Mary and his brothers James, Joseph, Simon and Judas? And aren't all his sisters here with us? Where does he get all this from?". Ah but we know better.. we know him.. So they turned against him.

Jesus' comment: "A prophet is not without honour, except in his home town and in his own family".

It hurts to be rejected by people you know and love.

But it gets worse. Desperate news arrives that his cousin John, John the Baptist, has been executed in jail by King Herod. Unjustly.

All this, by the way, you can read about in Matthew's Gospel.

After these knocks, Jesus is feeling pretty fragile - and he heads off across Lake Galilee into the hills for a break. For some peace and quiet. But his hiding place is rumbled and the crowds follow him. How can he turn them away? A large crowd, hungry to know the meaning of life. A crowd full of If onlys and Oh wows – and probably a few sceptical Ah buts among them, people who are dissatisfied with the way things are, who want change, who long for a fresh start.. but in many cases, they're not sure what they can do to make that change happen. They feel trapped. So they're listening hard. Maybe this guy really has got something to say. Perhaps he can give us real hope..

And doesn't time pass when you're enjoying yourself! Evening is drawing on and it's a remote area, so Jesus' followers, the disciples, have a bright idea.

"This is a remote place and the day has gone; send the people off to the villages to buy themselves food..".

Jesus has other plans and, starting with just 5 loves and 2 fishes, somehow feeds the lot of them – 5000 men and their families.

By now, Jesus is really is ready for a rest. And, if you're a fan of Strictly Come Dancing, it's a case of Nice to see you, to see you.. [nice]! Now, off home with you.

Jesus desperately needs some time to himself. So he sends the disciples back across the lake in their boat and goes into the hills to pray.

We were visiting our son and family in Clearwater, Florida in August. Fantastic beaches, beautiful sunshine.. until about 4 in the afternoon, when the clouds roll in, the thunder and lightning start and then comes the rain. There were three hurricanes threatening while we were there.. fortunately, none hit Florida.

And as Jesus prays and rests in the hills, the poor guys in their boat – Peter, James, John, Andrew, Nathaniel, Levi, If only, Ah but, Oh wow and the rest are battling with a head wind and rough sea. It's really late, they're pretty exhausted, it's after 3 in the morning - but it's starting to look pretty dodgy for them. They're in that desperate state of struggling with fatigue and almost despair.. when, as they heave up and down, one of them, If only, spots something through the dark and waves and spray:

"What's that?"
"What's what?"
"That, that over there.. coming towards us.. It's.. it's a ghost.."
"Oh wow…"
"It is, it's a ghost.."
"Ah but.. if it was a ghost, it would.."
"If only.. if only it was Jesus.. he'd help us.."
Oh wow! It is. "It's ok. Don't be afraid. It's me".

Ah but's brother, Yeah right is in the boat and peering into the darkness.

"Yeah, right. If it is you, Lord, tell me to come to you over the water".
"OK Peter, come on.."

And Peter steps out of the boat and onto the surface of the water, and walks towards Jesus.

Ah but has just turned into Oh wow. So has If only.

"But when Peter saw the strength of the gale he was afraid..".

Peter was quite a guy. He wore his heart on his sleeve. He was the leader, the most volatile, the one who either got things absolutely right.. or completely wrong. He's an emotional and impulsive person – it's not everyone who'd step out of a boat into the water in the middle of the night in thunder and lightning, in the midst of a hurricane.

Peter, by the way, was Jesus' right hand man. Jesus' rock. "On this rock", said Jesus, "I will build my Church".

Now. What do rocks do in water?

Peter's just remembered. "And beginning to sink, he cried 'Save me, Lord'. And at once, Jesus reached out and caught hold of him".

It's not really surprising that the Church today is full of If onlys, Ah buts and Oh wows.. The country is in a parlous state. Economic crisis. Jobs lost. Serious insecurity. Worries about where the money will come from to get by. People losing their homes. What about our youngsters, the hardest hit group, with youth unemployment seriously high and graduate unemployment pretty desperate. Then there are health problems and crime problems and alongside this we're involved in a war we aren't winning in Afghanistan and we're desperately concerned about the environment and.. and things, you could say, look pretty bleak.

No wonder If only and Ah but are having a field day. They've been proved right. The world is going to the dogs and there's nothing to be done.

Unless, like Peter, you're up for a bit of a challenge.

You may have an ailing parent, a failing family, a wild child, a rotten job, a lot of complex problems or issues you just can't avoid.. You may feel that life is out of control and the world is destroying itself and there's no realistic hope of anything ever changing.. You may feel alone, isolated and wish there were some friends around..

.. Jesus is saying to you – "Come". Step out in faith. Stop worrying. Take the risk. Step out of the boat and into the water. And when you struggle, or fall, or sink, reach out.. and you'll find his hand already reaching out to you.

Just a final comment. I was contacted indirectly last week by a woman with three small children. She is an Afghan Christian, living in Afghanistan. Her life is seriously at risk. Converting from Islam to become a Christian is a capital offence in Afghanistan and she could be hanged for it. And she is fearful that the secret police are on to her. She is one of a community of an estimated 5000 Afghan Christians in her area. 5000 secret believers willing to risk their lives for their faith.

Following Jesus – taking that step of faith - is no easy option. It's a commitment to follow in the steps of One who gave his life in order to sort out the mess the world is in. Stepping out of the boat also means being willing to rock the boat, to struggle for goodness and justice and love, to resist the cynicism of the Ah buts, to challenge the If onlys to action, to earth the Oh wows in reality.

The great thing about the Church is this: when you take that step of faith, you're surrounded by a bunch of pretty ordinary people, people just like us, people who try and fail, who mess up again and again, who aspire to greatness and still fall flat on their faces.. but people who know that, together, inspired by our vision of God and filled with the energy and life of Jesus, together.. together, we can – and will – change the world.. and make it more like it should be, a world of peace and justice, generosity and gentleness, respect and love. Each of us is special to God. And with a unique contribution to make. Each of us is vital to God's great plan. Ordinary people with an extra-ordinary calling.

The traditional title given to this story is Jesus walks on the water. Better would be Peter walks on the water. Or Peter's step of faith. Or even One small step for man, one big step for mankind. Or something simple like Just do it!

That's the message for each one of us today is this: Just do it! Be extra-ordinary. Take the step. Trust God.. and together let's change the world.

EASTER SUNDAY. ST MICHAEL'S CHURCH, WOBURN SANDS. 24 April 2011

I've often fancied becoming a script writer and the sad death yesterday of John Sullivan, who wrote things like *Only Fools and Horses,* made me look again at some of the books I have on script writing – *The Screenwriter's Problem Solver, Writing Dialogue for Scripts* and (my favourite) *How to Write a Movie in 21 Days.*

That last book taught me that you should have short scenes and break your movie down into a series of little bits:

• An exciting start – you must capture the audience in the first 3 minutes or you've lost them for ever..
• Crisis - after 30 minutes, it's clear that there is a challenge, a crisis, which our hero can't avoid..

• After 60 minutes, everything's gone wrong. Things look so bleak for our hero that there seems to be no hope left...
• And then, in the final 30 minutes, things come good so that, by 90 minutes, all is sorted out, the baddies have been routed and our hero is victorious.

What you should do is sit with a pen and paper and watch a popular, successful film, writing down every scene change. If you want a blow by blow account of *Robin Hood Prince of Thieves*, see me afterwards.

All the rules are broken in *Jesus the Movie*.

The story opens in the hubbub of a crowded and jostling Bethlehem at census time and a young mother gives birth in a stable in some back street, in unsanitary conditions, surrounded by animals. A few visitors somehow discover what's happened and come to visit. And then, the child and his family disappear – literally – as refugees to neighbouring Egypt, fearing the madness of the local King, and we hear almost nothing of them for some years.

They reappear, living quietly in the north of Judaea and – not for the next 30 minutes but the next 30 years – Jesus gets on with living and working and studying. He launches his life's work in his home village, Nazareth, with disastrous results. He stands up in the local synagogue and reads the passage set for that day. And then he identifies himself with the words of Israel's greatest prophet, Isaiah –

"The spirit of the Lord has.. sent me to announce good news to the poor, to proclaim release for prisoners and recovery of sight for the blind; to let the broken victims go free, to proclaim the year of the Lord's favour.". He rolled up the scroll, gave it back to the attendant and sat down. And all eyes in the synagogue were fixed on him. He began to address them:"'Today", he said, "in your hearing this text has come true" [Luke 4, 18, 19]. The listeners are so incensed they almost physically pick Jesus up and throw him out, down a steep hill where the synagogue stands [v 29].

Jesus' words may sound uncontroversial to us today, but for Jesus' contemporaries, what he is saying is deeply insulting, nothing short of blasphemy. He is equating himself to the saviour of the nation, the Messiah, the one so desperately awaited, the one who will free the people from the oppressive Roman rulers who have conquered their country.

We see the same kind of feeling in Libya, Syria, Bahrain and across the Middle East at this very moment. People rising up against the tyranny and oppression of their rulers. In the Holy Land itself, ironically, the Palestinians feel that they are under a yoke of oppression from Israel, the descendants of the very people so oppressed and abused by the Romans two thousand years earlier..

Think of our movie script again. We're now into the middle phase, minutes 30 to 60. And, let me tell you, it's going to end badly.

Jesus sets about sharing his ideas in the towns and villages around the Galilee region. And soon there are huge crowds coming to see him and listen to what he has to say. He heals many sick people and helps many people suffering from physical infirmities and mental trauma. For some people, he's a great entertainer. For a few, he's becoming more than that. He is becoming their inspiration, the very source of life for them, he gives them meaning, he gives them hope..

But some people have had enough of this upstart young radical, who stirs up trouble wherever he goes. And do you know what the last straw is? He turns up in Jerusalem, in the Holy City itself, and the crowd go bananas, cheering and shouting for him and laying palms and their cloaks across the road and calling out "Blessed is he who comes in the name of the Lord.. Hosanna..!".

It's the last straw indeed. The religious leaders go to the Roman authorities and tell them they want rid of this radical or there'll be a revolution.

The first 30 minutes of the movie took 30 years. The next 30 took 3 years. The final 30 minutes take a week. A week of betrayal and loss. A week of increasing mental and physical agony. A week when even Jesus' closest friends disappear into the shadows in fear and the deepest despair.

You know the story. The PR men do their work so well. The crowd discover that their hero is really a rogue – out to disrupt their lives and lead them into unwinnable conflict against the Romans. Far from supporting him, they want well rid of him. Bide your time.. the time will come to rise up against Rome, but it's not yet.. and it's certainly not with that man.

It's obvious, isn't it? It is in everybody's best interests that peace should be maintained and stability preserved. The people's spokesmen – the religious leaders – urge the crowd to keep calm and wait for the right time; and they assure the Roman Governor, Pontius Pilate, that they can control the masses and things will be ok if he can just remove the troublemaker.

So, to keep the peace and for the general good of all, Jesus is removed and sent to be executed.

At the 90th minute, *Jesus the Movie* comes to a heart wrenching end. Our hero hangs slumped and crushed on a wooden cross, nailed there between two other poor victims of the cruellest and most humiliating form of execution ever created. May this be a lesson for you all – don't mess with Rome.. and, also, don't give the people false ideas about freedom., because this is how it ends.

There are indeed costs and consequences to everything we do. Some of history's greatest advocates of freedom have paid the price of their stance – think of Mahatma Ghandi or Martin Luther King, who lost their lives leading people to respond, non violently, to the oppressive rule under which their people lived. Think of Nelson Mandela, whose opposition to apartheid in South Africa led to his imprisonment for 27 years. Think now of so many poor people - mainly civilians, many of them children

– suffering and dying as they are caught up in the cross fire between Gaddafi and the rebels in Libya or shot by the soldiers of the Syrian regime.

Think more personally about our own lives.. All of us have to live with the consequences of our actions. And not one of us, in our heart of hearts, can honestly say that we have no regrets. Words said, deeds done – or left undone – sadness and pain and sorrow are part of human existence and experience. If only I'd behaved differently, if only I hadn't done that.. If only..

Jesus the Movie Part Two starts just before dawn in a garden. A woman walks slowly. You can tell from her gait that she is feeling pretty awful. Numb. Shoulders slumped, head down, shuffling feet.. It looks like the bottom has fallen out of her world. And so it has.. She reaches her destination, a tomb cut into the rock. She's come to pay her respects one last time.. to a man who changed her life. And whose body now lies here.

She reaches the tomb - and is shaken to the very core of her being. The stone across the entrance has been moved and the body is gone.

You know the rest of the story. I read it to you just now. Against all the odds, against everything that makes sense, that young man is back.. he's not dead, he's alive. His life shone such a beam into the souls of his contemporaries. His teachings and actions still reverberate around the world and bring hope in the most desperate of situations to people on the verge of despair.. His vision of a world at peace with itself – and his offer to us to discover peace for ourselves, freedom from the guilt that gnaws way in the pit of our stomachs because of the things we've done.

If human beings can connive together to destroy the greatest life ever lived – to remove so deliberately the one person whose love for others was so utterly selfless – then how can they ever be forgiven? If we can mess up in our own lives – and let's be honest, there are so many things we could have done differently and better – and still be offered the chance to start again.. what does it take?

Mary of Magdala was the woman in the garden. Tradition has it that she was a woman of the streets, unclean, beyond redemption.. till she met Jesus and her life was changed forever.

Such is God's sense of humour, it was a reformed prostitute who was the first to meet the risen Christ.

If you're absolutely content with your life and have never done anything to upset or damage anyone else.. then I really can't recommend you go and see *Jesus the Movie Part Two*.

But if you know you've messed up and you want a fresh start, today – and you want to do your bit to make things right in your life and relationships, and the world a better place, then I have some good news for you: it's a big cast and they don't want celebrities to star, just people like you and me, with the experience of living and a real wish to give the performance of their life. Whatever the cost.

Jesus the Movie Part Two. In the struggle for good, He offered them life – and they never looked back.

MIDNIGHT MASS 2012. ST MICHAEL'S CHURCH, WOBURN SANDS 24 December 2012

We're delighted to welcome you to St Michael's Church this Christmas. We hope you'll be feeling warm and comfortable – during the summer, we changed the heating system, replacing oil and hot air with gas and radiators.

The cold weather is a real burden for many people in our country. Bills are shooting up, thousands are living in hostels and temporary accommodation, and the growth of rough sleepers in the past couple of years has been alarming. The Churches and community of Woburn Sands, with others in the Milton

Keynes area, are involved through the winter in providing shelter for homeless people. We thank God and pray for all those who volunteer and those who need at this time the help and shelter being offered.

Mary, far from home and struggling to find a place to rest, was heavily pregnant and desperate for somewhere to stop, where she could give birth. We know the story so well – and yet the circumstances of Jesus' birth continue down the ages to disturb us. How come the King of Kings, the Lord of Lords, the Prince of Peace should arrive to save the world in so unbecoming a manner?

The wonder of the Nativity scene must always be tempered with the squalor of the stable.

You may spot in Church an 'alternative' Nativity scene this Christmas. The familiar figures of the Holy Family of Bethlehem, the animals, the Wise Men, carved out of olive wood by Palestinian Christians, are divided by a great wall. A barrier to worship. A barrier to welcome. The wall which now divides Bethlehem is part of the separation barrier Israel began building in the West Bank in 2002, ostensibly to protect Jewish territory from Palestinian attacks.

The Amos Trust is the charity which has produced this Nativity scene.

"Today", the Trust says, " the 'little town of Bethlehem' lies behind a separation wall, an eight metre high concrete wall, built by the Israeli occupation forces. If Jesus was born today in Bethlehem, the Wise Men would spend several hours queuing to enter the town. As local residents of Bethlehem, the shepherds would have had much of their land confiscated for illegal Israeli settlements, and with a lack of freedom to travel and restrictions on trade, it would be very difficult for them to make a living as shepherds…".

This Christmas, we are right to remember those in our own community and country in need of homes and jobs. We should remember, too, the chaos and agony of the Middle East and especially of the people of Israel and surrounding area, Israelis, Palestinians, Syrians, Egyptians and so many more – caught up in a seemingly never ending cycle of violence and despair.

On our own, we won't make much difference to the world's problems – but together, prayerful and courageous in the face of selfishness and cynicism, we can make things change.

It's worth just reminding ourselves of just how radical, how unthinkable that passage I read from St John's Gospel must have sounded to John's contemporaries. It uses a popular concept of the time, the idea of the Logos, the Word, being the creative force behind the world, the universe, everything.

God speaks - and things happen. ".. all things were made through him and without him was not anything made that was made. In him was life…".

Greek was the most widely spoken language around the Middle East of Jesus' day… but it was Roman imperial rule that most people were subject to. The Roman Emperor was a great man-made god - to be worshipped by all under his rule. Julius Caesar was the first emperor to be divinized, Augustus followed and then all the Caesars, some of them deeply cruel and completely mad.

So here's the great contradiction… a great man-made-god is trumped by a great God made man.

The Word became flesh and dwelt among us.. and not just among us as a mighty King but as a poor, helpless baby born in poverty.

The first challenge comes to the puppet King of Judaea, Herod the Great. So great, he's terrified by rumours of a rival, albeit a baby rival.. and sends his soldiers out to destroy all the boys under 3 they can find around Bethlehem. Just to make sure. To this King, human life has no value. Nor does it to that agent of the Empire, Pontius Pilate, 30 years later. He knows Jesus is innocent. He knows he has done nothing wrong. Yet he still allows him to be executed, crucified.

When the Word becomes flesh, expect surprises. For out of this life, and death, has come such change that, 2000 years later, the Roman Empire and many more empires have been and gone.. and still the Prince of Peace is worshipped by many millions of people across the world.

The Gospel – the Good News – of Jesus Christ is this: things can be different. Because the Bethlehem baby was to live a life of such love and truth that politics and religion, those great burdens which promise so much and deliver so little, couldn't stand having the light shone on them and had to get rid of him.

Was that the end? No. God raised Jesus from death and his presence, his power to bring hope out of despair, his overwhelming love for us is there for us to receive and live.

This Christmas, let's pray for one another and support each other as, together, we work for real and lasting change, to the benefit of all.

I wish you a very happy Christmas. And may God bless you this coming year.

CHAPTER 12

ST PAUL THE ENTREPRENEUR

My intention during my time on sabbatical was to explore the idea of 'St Paul the entrepreneur'. Maybe that's an attempt to impose on a man who lived two thousand years ago a rather modern, Western take on life. It highlights the problem of hermeneutics – how to understand and interpret what was written 2000 years ago, in a very different culture and context. I'll come back to it shortly.

Professor John Barclay, the Durham academic with whom I discussed this in late January 2013, didn't rubbish the idea, which was good of him. He suggested books which dug deep into St Paul's thinking and writing, including one by a Catholic theologian, Jerome Murphy-O'Connor (*Paul: A Critical Life*. OUP 1996), who has also written a biography of St Paul: *Paul: His Story* (OUP 2004).

I warmed to Murphy-O'Connor's style and the way he dealt with Paul's controversial and explosive relationship with the great Apostle Peter. It all came to a head over circumcision – should Gentile (non-Jewish) Christian converts be made to follow Jewish practises and be circumcised? Should they be required to eat only appropriate, kosher food? Should Christianity be understood as the fulfilment of Jewish faith and hope or a faith for all peoples everywhere?

"Evidently", writes Murphy-O'Connor about Paul's communication to the Thessalonians, "he [Paul] was much more concerned with what the community did than what it thought, and had worked out a strategy in advance. From the beginning, he realised that if the Thessalonian Church was to have the sort of witness value that would reinforce and prolong his mission, its members would have to exhibit an attractive, freely chosen lifestyle" (*Paul: A Critical Life* p 129).

I quickly began to discover other books, written mainly in the last two decades, which proved not only informative but powerfully enlightening. Of course, all historical and theological study is subject to interpretation. One of the books I found most compelling – brilliantly written and powerfully persuasive – was *The Messiah and the Kingdom. How Jesus and Paul ignited a revolution and transformed the world* (Grosset Putnam1997) by American theologian Richard Horsley and historian and archaeologist Neil Asher Silberman.

> History has always been written from the viewpoint of those who build cities and conquer empires, but in the New Testament and the early Christian tradition we may be able to catch a rare glimpse at the hopes, dreams, and utopian visions of those who suddenly find themselves at the bottom of a new civilisation's social heap. In this book, we will argue that earliest Christianity was a movement that boldly challenged the heartlessness and arrogance of a vast governmental bureaucracy – run on unfairly apportioned tax burdens and guided by cynical special interests – that preached about 'opportunity', 'self reliance', and 'personal achievement' while denying all three to the vast majority of men, women and children over whom it presumed to rule (p 5).

Different theologians, in their detailed examination of biblical texts and other ancient manuscripts, archaeological evidence and contemporary information from history and philosophy, attempt to identify not only what might have been the original sayings of Jesus and traditions of the early Christians, but also what might genuinely have been dictated by Paul and what, with his name attached, might actually have been drafted some time later by his followers. Their arguments often surmise that the Pauline letters we have in our Bibles today are, in some cases, conflations of different letters. Take, for example, the letter to the Philippians: "Some commentators distinguish two letters." says Murphy-O'Connor, "The majority detect three letters. But there have always been those who maintain the unity of the epistle" (p 215). For those of us who are not academic theologians, getting back to the original intent of the writer(s) is not easy!

The First Paul – reclaiming the radical visionary behind the Church's conservative icon (SPCK 2009), is a good example of this process of examination and interpretation. The American authors, Marcus Borg and John Dominic Crossan, entitle their first chapter *Paul: Appealing or Appalling?* They go on to argue that there are three Pauls:

• the author of seven 'genuine' letters (Romans, 1 and 2 Corinthians, 1 Thessalonians, Galatians, Philippians, Philemon), himself the original 'radical' Saul of Tarsus;
• a later author, writing some decades after the death of St Paul, of 1 and 2 Timothy and Titus - the 'reactionary' Paul;
• a collection of letters of disputed authorship, Ephesians, Colossians and 2 Thessalonians – by the 'conservative' Paul.

Borg and Crossan differ from Murphy-O'Connor, Horsley and Silberman and others in deciding which letters they attribute to the original Paul and which are written later by others in the 'Pauline school'. Borg is an academic of Lutheran origin, who worked for many years at Oregon State University, retiring in 2007, when he became the canon theologian at Trinity Episcopal Cathedral in Portland, Oregon). Crossan is a Catholic New Testament scholar and former priest now living in Orlando, Florida since retiring from academic life. Both have been involved for many years in work on The Jesus Seminar, exploring and trying to understand in their context the biblical writings and other early sources of information about Jesus and the early Church – trying to get back to the 'Jesus of history'.

THE JESUS OF HISTORY

I have always had a soft spot for Albert Schweitzer, the great early 20th century theologian and missionary of Lambarene in the Gambia, West Africa, whose famous book *The Quest of the Historical Jesus*, first published in 1906, concluded that Jesus will always be a foreigner to us: "the historical Jesus will be to our time a stranger and an enigma".

Schweitzer was a brilliant theologian and outstanding organist. But he packed it all in, trained to be a doctor and spent the rest of his life in Africa. The term he used to sum up his world view was 'respect for life'. In his book *The Philosophy of Civilization* (first published in 1923), he wrote that "true philosophy" begins with the idea that "I am a life that wants to live, in the midst of life that wants to live" (from Chapter 26, *The Ethics of Reverence for Life*).

Schweitzer the Western missionary was wrestling with the challenge of 'practising Jesus' in a context and situation vastly different to everything he had previously known. So trying to get to the heart of what it really means to 'practise Jesus' – my words, not his – was of ultimate significance. A description from one of his African colleagues, Gustave, is interesting:

> "The importance of Jesus Christ to mankind", Dr. Schweitzer explained, "does not lie in the rituals people have made out of his teaching, but in the example of his life. His love and compassion and his willingness to die for the conviction that his death would redeem all men from suffering and sin, these are the deeds that have been remembered throughout time..".
> (recorded by Louise Jilek-Aall in *Working with Doctor Schweitzer*, her account of life at Lambarene in 1961. Online edition http://www.mentalhealth.com/books/lja/lja-toc.html).

The former Bishop of Durham, Tom Wright, in *What St Paul Really Said* (Lion Hudson 1997), begins with a survey of the leading 20th century theologians studying Paul - and Schweitzer is first in his list (pp 12ff). For Schweitzer, Wright says, "Paul is Jewish through and through, even though, precisely through his work as the Jewish apostle to the Gentiles, he prepared the way for the subsequent Hellenisation of Christianity" (p 13).

Back to another prominent author, Wayne Meeks, whose *The First Urban Christians: The Social World of the Apostle Paul* (Yale

University Press, 1983) has been influential for 30 years in this area of scholarship.

He and other scholars make the point that Paul's early writings (the 'radical' Paul) appear quite soon after the death and resurrection of Jesus. Most scholars think that Paul's first letter to the Thessalonians was written within 20 years of Jesus' death, around 52AD. Paul's early letters pre-date the Gospels and are therefore the earliest authentic clues to what the first followers of Jesus really believed and how they lived.

> From both the letters and Acts it is evident that Pauline Christianity was not the work of a single person, but of an extended group of associates... the Pauline association was a self-conscious movement which accorded to Paul the position of 'founder' or leading authority (Meeks, pp 7, 8).

Meeks, in agreeing with other scholars that the Pauline letters are not all by Paul the Apostle, states that they (and some other slightly later writings) "all represent a slow development in which the figure of Paul was adopted as a patron". And not just this. Paul and his associates seem to have operated mainly in cities. Pauline Christianity

> stood on the growing edge of the Christian movement, for it was in the cities of the Roman Empire that Christianity, though born in the village culture of Palestine, had its greatest successes until well after the time of Constantine (p 8).

Meeks goes on to describe the ways in which Paul and his associates would engage with people in the cities they visited. Paul was a superlative networker and used his contacts very effectively. The early Christian communities were a mix of people from different social classes. Paul was adept at making his message fit the circumstances of the towns he worked in. His new 'assemblies' were in the tradition of what Horsley and Silberman call the Jewish 'reform communities' Jesus had started in Galilee.

Paul took patronage seriously and recognised the benefit of having the support and involvement of people with high social standing in the community – though he constantly challenged the assumption that class discrimination and power relationships were impossible to change.

Paul Skirrow, responding to an early draft of this chapter and commenting on Meeks' assertion, makes the point that,

> in terms of taking patronage seriously, it is important to remember how Jesus systematically attacked and undermined the patron-client system, as well as other social structures such as kinship, the marginalisation of women, the right of men to divorce women, kingship, the power of the ideology manufacturers in the temple, etc (unpublished correspondence, February 2013).

Paul's radical message (in the early letters) was that everyone, men and women, even slaves, were equal before God and therefore equal in the Christian community. So, the challenge, as Borg and Crossman state it, is this: "

> The only way to understand a Pauline letter is to turn it into a Pauline story by working our way through the Pauline matrix of a single letter within all his other letters within Diaspora Judaism within the Roman Empire (p 30).

PAUL AND SLAVERY

Borg and Crossan's piecing together of the story behind the short, one chapter letter of the 'radical' Paul to Philemon makes for an intriguing read. Philemon is a Christian of high standing whose runaway slave, Onesimus, has ended up in Rome with Paul. "I am appealing to you [Philemon] for my child Onesimus, whose father I have become during my imprisonment..." (Philemon verses 8 – 9). Paul's point is this: he, Philemon and Onesimus are all in it together, all brothers in Christ. So, says Paul, I'm not keeping Onesimus with me, I'm sending him back to you. But not as your slave – as your brother in Christ.

> Onesimus' liberation could not have been kept a secret. What if Philemon had other slaves – would there have been an immediate mass conversion to Christianity? What rumors would have spread throughout the slave infrastructure of their village or city about Christians – unfairly, but maybe inevitably – of advising slaves to flee their owners or maybe murder them in their beds. Still, even if granted all of that, it is still sad that the radical Paul of the letter to Philemon was so swiftly and thoroughly sanitised into the conservative Paul of Colossians and Ephesians.

> In both those books, pseudo-Paul addresses Christian slaves and Christian slave owners and thereby depicts those relationships as perfectly normal (p 45).

Horsley and Silberman sum up the Philemon/Onesimus situation by emphasising the significance of the imprisoned Paul's request:

> At stake in this request was Paul's newly focused social vision, which he maintained even as he languished in prison and his network of communities teetered on the verge of disintegration. To challenge the institution of slavery even among his most loyal supporters was, to his mind, the only effective way to strike a blow against Caesar. And even though the fate of his Galatian communities was now uncertain, Corinth seemed lost, and Macedonia might soon fall to his opponents, Paul had come to believe that in an age of patrons and clients, of power and exploitation, of status and possessions, only continual acts of radical self sacrifice, modelled on the crucified figure of Jesus Christ, could renew and redeem the world (p 183).

PAUL ON WOMEN

While visiting Durham, I spent time in the library of my old College, St John's, and there discovered an article on *Women as Leaders in the New Testament*. In it was a persuasive argument for seeing Paul's attitude to women in a quite different light to how it is generally understood. The writer speaks of a progressive development in Paul's thought as, over time, he became less radical: "the Pauline letters also display a progressive accommodation of the radical ideal to societal norms, culminating in the blanket prohibition of women's leadership in 1 Timothy" (p 15). But his early letters really are 'radical'.

> Far from being a utopian and impractical ideal, Paul's statement that "in Christ there is no male or female" was intended to have an impact on the day-to-day life of the Church. We can see evidence of its impact in the practise of the Pauline Churches, where women exercised a variety of roles that we would associate with Church leadership in the fields of stewardship, prophecy and the "ministry of the word". (*Women as Leaders in the New Testament, Modern Believing, in The Journal of Theological Liberalism*. p 15)

Murphy-O'Connor takes a similar line, stating that "Paul took it entirely for granted that women were ministers of the church in precisely the same way as men. He recognised their gifts as fruits of the Spirit." (p 289). This comes in his analysis of the Church in Corinth, where Paul was having (in the first letter to the Corinthians) to deal with a range of issues related to male-female relationships.

PAUL'S CHALLENGE TO HIS CONTEMPORARIES

The academics I have referred to are all attempting to explore Paul's thinking and teaching. They make clear the challenge he posed to his contemporaries – not just those he was seeking to convert but his fellow Christians, especially the Jewish Christians. Paul was certainly not afraid to call a spade a spade and his fury at what he sees as the betrayal of Peter and even Barnabas, his co-worker and probably his senior partner in the early years, is palpable.

Whether it was justified is another matter. One perspective on the Peter/Paul conflict, as articulated by Paul Skirrow, is that,

> with the fledgling faith becoming urbanised and, as a result, in the process of, or certainly at risk of, becoming Hellenised, there were issues about what might be gained or lost or changed. It is possible to suggest a theory that the debate between Paul (and others) and Peter (and others) was to do with the methods required to tackle the danger of losing the essence of the Gospel way of life, as it fell prey to external, imperialist, philosophical expressions, and being co-opted by the dominant classes. Peter offered a strategy which entailed pulling back as far as possible in order to retain authenticity, including hanging on to certain 'Jewish' practises, while Paul seemed to favour a more liberal approach.

> The above does not negate Murphy-O'Connor's views or those of other theologians but it suggests first we need to be aware of the complexities – Peter and Paul were fighting the same 'enemy', not each other, and it was not just about circumcision (unpublished correspondence, February 2013).

PAUL'S FIERCE INDEPENDENCE

Paul was probably only a few years younger than Jesus. There is no record of him ever having actually seen or met Jesus in the flesh, though, according to Luke's Acts of the Apostles, Paul, though born in Tarsus in Cilicia, grew up in Jerusalem, educated by Gamaliel as a Pharisee, full of zeal and, in time, an avid hunter-down and persecutor of members of the small but growing sect of followers of Jesus.

His dramatic conversion – a mystical encounter with the crucified and risen Jesus Christ on the Damascus road – was followed, Paul says in Galatians, by three years in the desert. I have always thought that most of that time must have been spent in prayer and meditation, preparing for his future apostolic ministry.

Borg and Crossan, Murphy-O'Connor, Meeks and others don't think that was how it happened. A few days of quiet perhaps, but it was not long before Paul was busily engaging with the local Nabatean Arab communities in the area. The city of Damascus was Paul's mission base and, say Borg and Crossan,

> at the very time that the Jewish Paul was conducting a mission to convert the Nabateans to Christian Judaism, their king was conducting a war to defeat the Jewish tetrarch Herod Antipas. When therefore Aretas acquired Damascus between 37 – 39CE, Paul's base in Arabia was now under his control and Paul's days were numbered (p 76).

Because he was Jewish, Paul had to get out of Damascus in a hurry. And that was when he was lowered down over the city wall – for fear of the Nabatean authorities, according to 2 Corinthians. Luke's account states (rather less credibly) that it was the Jews he was fleeing from.

Luke has it that Paul, after this first, unsuccessful missionary experience, heads off home to Tarsus, where he is tracked down and recruited by Barnabas, a prominent member of the Christian Jewish community in Antioch. It was in Antioch that the issue of Jewish and Gentile Christian practise had become urgent and needed to be addressed. The Antioch assembly ordered Barnabas and Paul – very much the junior partner – to go for advice to the mother Church in Jerusalem.

Acts 15 records their meeting with James, the brother of Jesus and Peter the Apostle. The agreement they reach is to allow Gentile converts to forego the need for circumcision or conformity to the rituals of Judaism, though they should refrain from eating food offered to idols and their moral behaviour should be exemplary. Meeks writes:

Paul finds it necessary to insist that the leaders "added nothing to me", except "Cephas [Peter], James and John" on the one side, Paul and Barnabas on the other, sealed by "the right hand of partnership".

The agreement was short lived. For a time the solidarity of Jew and Gentile in the Antioch groups was celebrated by common meals, in which even Peter, who had arrived from Jerusalem, participated. Yet when "certain persons from James" appeared, Peter and the other Jewish Christians except Paul – even Barnabas, his closest associate – withdrew from such meals, leaving Paul isolated" (Gal 2, 11 – 13; Meeks p 111).

Even Barnabas. Paul was gutted. His letter to the Galatians radiates the pain and anger he felt at such a betrayal. Paul's independence of thought and action, his willingness to go it alone in order to be true to himself and his calling, his conviction that he was right and the others were wrong – these are indeed characteristics of what we nowadays might call an entrepreneur.

Murphy-O'Connor, in *Paul, His Story*, sums up Paul's approach.

He would not give obedience to any law, and he would not exact submission from his converts to any precept, be it from God, Jesus, or himself. In consequence, he was strictly limited in his guidance of the community. He could indicate what he expected of its members. He could attempt to persuade them to modify their behavior. He could propose his own example ... But that was all! ... his experience at Antioch had taught Paul that to operate through binding precepts would necessarily bring him and his converts back into the orbit of the Law (p 132).

The book's Epilogue also offers an explanation for why Paul's version of practising Jesus was not entirely adopted:

The communities that Paul founded needed perhaps a generation to shake themselves free of his overwhelming background presence. Then they began to come to a true appreciation of his importance. This showed itself in a renewed appreciation of his letters. ... Thus communities carefully conserved what they had received, and requested those that he had sent to other churches (p 236).

THE LORDSHIP OF CHRIST

Paul was also provocative in the way he adapted existing, familiar concepts and slogans, turning them around and giving them new and profoundly different meanings. He would have been a modern advertising agency's dream. See, for example, Paul's teaching on the Lordship of Christ - fascinating when set in its historical and cultural context. Borg and Crossan explain this brilliantly.

> Augustus [the Roman Emperor] was Divine, Son of God, God, and God from God. He was Lord, Liberator, Redeemer, and Savior of the world... Words like 'justice' and 'peace', 'epiphany' and 'gospel', 'grace' and 'salvation' were already associated with him. Even 'sin' and 'atonement' were connected to him as well (p 93).

They then argue that Paul, in drawing on all these ideas and concepts, is utterly subversive – he works with those familiar ideas and all they imply, and just turns them upside down. Tom Wright, in *What St Paul Really Said*, also calls Paul subversive, and, commenting on Paul's famous passage in Philippians 2 ("every tongue shall confess that Jesus is Lord"), he writes:

> Paul's gospel was indeed a royal announcement.. 'Another King' – as Paul knew only too well, people tend to get put in prison for saying that sort of thing. We should not be surprised to discover that that was where Paul was when he wrote half of his letters (p 57).

Pax Romana was brought about by force. The strength of the Empire was what kept people in their place and ensured order and peace. It was a comprehensive, all-encompassing peace, reaching into every corner of life. Borg and Crossan stress this point:

> Think.. of those proclamations of imperial justice and peace that accompanied the accession of Nero as ipse Deus – 'a very God', or better, 'the God himself' – after his accession in 54 CE (p 96).

And think how Nero turned out.

The peace of Christ, however, was utterly different. And certainly not to be compartmentalised into applying only to the 'spiritual' bits of life.

> The problem for Rome was not calling others 'Lord' or even speaking of 'our Lord'. That could be quite ordinary, innocent and acceptable. But it was treasonous confrontation to claim that 'our Lord' was 'the Lord' (p 110).

> The crucial difference between the program of Caesar and the program of Christ is between peace through violent victory and peace through non-violent justice. Both promise peace on earth, so the confrontation is in means and not ends...

> Caesar not only proclaims but incarnates peace through violent victory, just as Christ not only proclaims but incarnates peace through non-violent justice. There will be peace on earth, said Roman imperial theology, when all is quiet and orderly. There will be peace on earth, said Pauline Christian theology, when all is fair and just (p 121).

Paul brilliantly turns upside down the whole basis for bringing peace to the world. No wonder he could write "The peace of God, which passes all understanding..." (Philippians 4, 7).

PAUL AND GRACE

Borg and Crossan make an interesting point in their opening chapter of *The First Paul*: that "Catholics and Protestants see Paul's importance quite differently" (p 5). Borg was raised a Lutheran, his understanding of the foundational Christian message being 'justification by grace through faith'. "Not until I went to seminary in my early twenties did I realize how Lutheran my way of seeing Paul and the gospel was", he writes (p 5).

The Catholic Crossan "grew up blissfully unaware of those battling interpretations of Paul or even the fierce Reformation controversies about him" (p 6). For Crossan, Peter and Paul were the twin heroes of Christian Rome, their respective roles illustrated in a 4th century lamp shaped like a boat, with Peter seated in the stern and Paul standing in the prow, looking forward. "Peter steers. Paul guides. And the boat sails full before the wind" (p 7).

The idea of the gift of Jesus, freely given to save undeserving sinners, is deeply embedded in my own psyche and that of many millions of Christians down the ages. It should go without saying that receiving the gift of God's grace is not the same as believing a set of propositions or dogmas. Believing the right things is not what Paul means by faith. In fact, Paul's thinking, following Jesus' teaching, is radically different to the prevailing culture and expectations of his contemporaries.

Skirrow and Winn, in their unpublished work on Matthew's Gospel, comment on Matthew 6, the Sermon on the Mount, that

> The wealthy and powerful do not behave justly and so do not know God. When they give alms they do not give to support those who struggle but in order to receive honour and acclaim. They give in an ostentatious manner so everyone knows who is the giver and who is the one who receives the gift. This sort of giving is not about generosity or justice but about securing honour and maintaining a hierarchical social order. When Jesus tells his audience that they should give their alms in secret he instructs them that their practise is to undermine the dominant social structure. Giving alms is about justice. It cannot be used to create debt and obligation or to sustain an unjust system (Paul

Skirrow and Peter Winn. Unpublished work on St Matthew's Gospel).

Jesus and Paul in their teaching were indeed radically opposite to the thinking of their contemporaries. John Barclay explores the ways in which, in diverse cultures throughout history, the idea of the 'gift' has not been thought of as an unconditional act of generosity. It comes with strings attached. Reciprocity is expected, not necessarily in the form of a gift back of equal or greater value, but in a range of ways, including what could be grovelling gratitude for patronage or in ensuring public honour and respect.

Barclay let me see the first chapter of a book he is writing on the subject. That chapter, entitled *The Anthropology and History of the Gift*, demonstrates how our modern, Western mind has come to perceive 'gift' and 'grace'. Barclay draws on the pioneer of the 16th century Reformation in Europe, the monk Martin Luther.

Martin Luther.. challenged the construction of human relations with God as a repeated cycle of gift-and-return, and thereby countered notions of human merit as eliciting benefits from God. Luther's theology is centrally about gift – the gift (grace) of God expressed definitively and once-for-all in the life, death and resurrection of God, and the gift/generosity of Christ passed on to others in free Christian service. Against a long-established tradition, Luther reconfigured the mass as the reception of grace in Word and sacrament, not a sacrifice offered to God in the hope of obtaining divine benefits (for oneself or for others). God, in other words, gives freely and without strings attached, and believers are to do likewise.

Luther places much emphasis on imitation of Christ or, better, participation in the dynamic of the Christ-event: believers are to be (as he puts it) 'Christs' to one another, passing on the unconditional love of Christ to others.. Gift-giving is, in other words, a pure, gratuitous act, liberated from the need to gain anything by the fact that Christ has given all things already, and freed from a self-seeking attitude by pure concern for the other.

Luther's theology was honed in the face of huge opposition from the medieval Church. It challenged the corrupt power of popes, bishops and clergy and made Jesus Christ freely accessible to all. Luther taught that 'Law' shows up our sinfulness, God's grace lifts the burden of sin and sets us free – and then Law shows us how to live.

Luther drew heavily on the writings of St Paul and the teaching of Paul's great 5th century successor, St Augustine of Hippo.

Augustine was living in the final days of the Roman Empire. The Goths were coming, an unstoppable force that soon would destroy civilisation. Augustine knew it – and, not surprisingly, his outlook was pretty bleak. His pessimistic view of human nature reflected such bleakness – and Luther, like Augustine, taught that humanity could do nothing good, nothing right, without the grace of God.

Both Augustine and Luther held that there were two spheres of God's activity. Augustine spoke of the City of God and the City of the world. Luther spoke of two 'Kingdoms', spiritual and secular. Both were under God's rule.

> We are to be subject to governmental power and do what it bids, as long as it does not bind our conscience but legislates only concerning outward matters…But if it invades the spiritual domain and constrains the conscience, over which God only must preside and rule, we should not obey it at all but rather lose our necks. Temporal authority and government extend no further than to matters which are external and corporeal (Martin Luther, *Secular Authority: to what extent it should be obeyed*. See John Dillenberger, *Martin Luther. Selections from his writings*. A Doubleday Anchor Original 1961 pp364ff).

Lutheran theology – or practise – rooted in the doctrine of the Two Kingdoms was to be found severely wanting in the mid 20th century when Adolf Hitler came to power in Germany. As aggressive secular forces became increasingly demonic in the proclamation of Aryan superiority and treatment of Jews, gypsies and other minorities, the weak and compromised German Lutheran Church – and the Catholic Church – proved powerless to oppose them.

A great hero of mine has always been the Lutheran theologian Dietrich Bonhoeffer, a brilliant young German pastor who became involved in the failed bomb plot to destroy the Führer. Bonhoeffer was arrested and imprisoned before being executed. Not only was he a brave and committed man who knowingly compromised his fundamental belief in the sanctity of life (by trying to kill another human being, Adolf Hitler) for the greater good, he was also a bold thinker, not afraid to wrestle with the meaning of Christian faith in a modern world vastly different to the world of Jesus and the early Church.

SO WHAT'S LAW FOR?

One of my great frustrations is how stupid Governments can be. Their responsibility for framing good laws is of profound importance, but, too often, we are saddled not with grace-ful laws which make us want to behave better, but with ill thought out, grace-less laws which we try to find ways around.

So, for a start, we need a fresh approach to Law. Doesn't the 'spirit' of the Law matter more than the 'letter'? Paul seemed to think so. The spirit of the Law has to do with setting frameworks for good behaviour but the letter of the Law thinks it can just legislate and regulate good behaviour into existence – and fails miserably. You can't just create new laws and expect people to behave well. Some are so adept at finding ways of getting round the regulations. Others shrivel under the regulatory burden.

What we need is to develop the concept of 'grace-ful living' – and 'grace-ful Law'. Law in the Old Testament is not a set of regulations drawn up by misery guts determined to spoil our fun, but a framework for living wholesome and healthy lives, together, in community. This is entirely in the spirit of Pauline thinking and fits well with the idea of practising Jesus.

In the early 1990s, I was seconded to the Government and used to have to draft speeches for Ministers. In one speech – which was used in Huddersfield and so went on the record – the Minister, Robin Squire, described the purpose of Government as follows:

- •To promote the common good,
- •To prevent wrongdoing, and
- •To protect the poor and weak.

Ideas taken straight out of the Old Testament and built on in the Gospels, where Jesus explains that he is not about abolishing the Law but fulfilling it. The Law, says Jesus, is all about loving God and loving your neighbour as yourself. Love, says St Paul, is the fulfilment of the Law (Romans 13.10). The context in which Paul says this is his section on Church and State – how to live Christianly in society.

Neil Elliot, in his opening remarks in *Liberating Paul. The justice of God and the politics of the apostle* (Maryknoll, New York 1994), spells out ways in which Paul's letters have been misused to justify a multitude of social evils down the ages. One of the sub-headings in his opening chapter is *The Pauline legacy as an ideological weapon of death* (p 9). He continues:

> Paul is in chains today, a slave of Death.. Why is Paul so easily accommodated to the dynamics of oppression and death? (p 19).. I am convinced, and mean to convince my reader, that Paul himself is far more an advocate of human liberation than the inherited theological tradition has led us to think (p 23).

Elliot's case is that the worst-used bits of Paul, the ones that have served to legitimise structures of injustice, are actually the later, "'pseudonymous' letters, that is in letters not written by Paul himself" (p 21). This is a similar argument to that presented by Borg and Crossan and others.

PAUL THE ENTREPRENEUR

I think of myself as a (not very good) entrepreneur – to be more precise, a social entrepreneur. I've never been much cop at making money but I do have ideas and like to try and turn them into practical actions. Some of them are described in earlier chapters. I remember attending an event in New Zealand House in Central London 12 years ago and the person at reception produced a badge for me to wear. "How shall I describe you on the badge?" she asked. "What about 'social entrepreneur'?" I replied – at which she burst into laughter. The term was not very familiar then. Nowadays it is widely used.

I love the definition of 'social entrepreneur' on the Ashoka website. I know Ashoka well, having shared office space some years ago with this innovative international agency for radical change in society.

> Social entrepreneurs are individuals with innovative solutions to society's most pressing social problems. They are ambitious and persistent, tackling major social issues and offering new ideas for wide-scale change.

> Rather than leaving societal needs to the government or business sectors, social entrepreneurs find what is not working and solve the problem by changing the system, spreading the solution and persuading entire societies to take new leaps.

> Social entrepreneurs often seem to be possessed by their ideas, committing their lives to changing the direction of their field. They are both visionaries and ultimate realists, concerned with the practical implementation of their vision above all else.

> Each social entrepreneur presents ideas that are user-friendly, understandable, ethical, and engage widespread support in order

to maximize the number of local people that will stand up, seize their idea, and implement with it. In other words, every leading social entrepreneur is a mass recruiter of local changemakers—a role model proving that citizens who channel their passion into action can do almost anything.

Over the past two decades, the citizen sector has discovered what the business sector learned long ago: there is nothing as powerful as a new idea in the hands of a first-class entrepreneur.

Paul was an innovator, ambitious and persistent and certainly offering new ideas for wide-scale change. He wasn't the kind of person to wait around for others to solve problems. And, without a doubt, he was, as it were, a man possessed. His thinking was coloured by his expectation that God would, very soon, bring about the end of the world and the Messiah, Jesus, would return (see 1 Thessalonians 4, 15 – 17, 1 Corinthians 15, 51 – 52). He was a visionary, yes. But utterly, urgently pragmatic. And he was to prove, in time, to be perhaps the world's leading mass recruiter of local changemakers!

Paul maintained his own independence of thought and action throughout his Christian mission and ministry. Summoned to Jerusalem to meet with James the brother of Jesus, Peter the Apostle and others of the original Christian community, he seems to have accepted their authority and agreed to their (pretty moderate) requirements – so there was no loss of face on either side. But, having gone along with whatever they said, he then went away and did his own thing.

And, as it turned out, "there is nothing as powerful as a new idea in the hands of a first-class entrepreneur".

I think Paul was also an opportunist. He had a broad vision, a long term goal – and he knew that, in Christ, he could do anything. So, when opportunities arose, the chances are he would respond. And when doors closed, he'd either move on or find another way round the obstacle.

RESONANCES WITH PAUL

So, what are the characteristics of Paul which resonate with me?

I recognise in myself someone who is happier starting things than continuing and sustaining them. I acknowledge an impatience in myself which can make me unwilling to persist with doing things which seem to be immovable or unshakeable – I'd rather find a way round or through the obstacles. I find it hard to understand people who can't think 'outside the box' or 'on their feet' and become impatient.

I have used phrases to describe myself – 'going for the gaps' and 'minding other people's business' – which are supposed to be light-hearted and amusing but actually contain a glimmer of truth. I often find myself tending to 'overstate the case to make the point'. I like big challenges and am always in danger of being caught up in my latest Big Project. I'm not just a 'big picture' person –– but I am happier with dreaming the dreams than dealing with the minutiae, though I can when I have to. Having said that, I'm at my most pedantic when proof reading. I hate mis-spellings and wrong punctuation, even though I get things wrong myself.

What I particularly enjoy is networking – that's the bit about 'minding other people's business'! I enjoy making connections between disparate people and groups. One of the projects I was involved with, described in Chapter 4, was called Linking Up Inter-Faith. Actually, the title wasn't one that I dreamed up. The credit for it should go to Malcolm Brown, now Secretary to the Division for Mission and Public Affairs in the Church of England's General Synod. Linking Up's work involved networking across the country and connecting people and projects. I make no claims to be a "mass recruiter of local changemakers" but I am encouraged by the changemakers among the networks I am involved with.

That Ashoka quote - "there is nothing as powerful as a new idea in the hands of a first-class entrepreneur" - I find somewhat daunting. I love new ideas and, although I can claim absolutely no new or completely original idea as my own, I do like to take the ideas of others and put them together, sometimes in quite new ways. And, maybe, that was what Paul did - picking up the Gospel threads already in common practise and parlance.

One thing is certain - despite all the problems he encountered and opposition he faced, even within his own Christian networks, Paul remained convinced of the importance of his own calling and message. Loveday Alexander, in a conference address to St Albans Diocesan clergy (June 2012), unpacked Paul's first letter, 1 Thessalonians, calling it his 'base camp'.

She used a simple triangular model (contained within a circle, representing the world) to describe the relationship between God (point A), Church (point B) and apostolic leadership (point C). God calls and empowers A - B and A - C. Too much emphasis on B - C (a feature of much thinking about leadership in today's Church) actually misses the point that Paul spent only a few weeks in Thessalonica before being forced to leave and that infant assembly was left, therefore, to stand on its own feet.

THE TIPPING POINT

One of my favourite books is Malcolm Gladwell's *The Tipping Point* (Little, Brown and Company 2000). I found it in a (now defunct) Borders bookshop and read it right through there and then. I bought it and re-read it and, every so often, go back to it. Gladwell refines the idea of 'networking' in Chapter 2, *The Law of the Few* (pp 31 - 88) on 'connectors', 'mavens' and 'salesmen'. He uses the example of Paul Revere, whose famous midnight ride through the local villages and communities around Boston alerted the colonial settlers to the British army's plan to march on Lexington and arrest the colonial leaders.

Revere, says Gladwell, is his archetypal Connector. But he didn't just pass on information – he somehow created a social epidemic, a response which led to mass action. Gladwell contrasts this with another fellow revolutionary, William Dawes, who, like Revere, set out at the same time on another route to Lexington to warn the colonials of the oncoming British force. For some reason, his message made minimal impact and few people turned out from the villages he visited along his route to resist the British.

"What makes someone a Connector?" asked Gladwell. "The first – and most obvious – criterion is that Connectors know lots of people.. Sprinkled among every walk of life.. are a handful of people with a truly extraordinary knack of making friends and acquaintances. They are Connectors" (p 38).

Gladwell suggests that the reason for Paul Revere's success – how he started a 'word of mouth epidemic' – was that "He was a Connector. He was, for example, gregarious and intensely social.. with an 'uncanny genius for being at the center of events'" (p 56).

There are echoes of St Paul in this idea of a 'connector' being someone who doesn't just pass on information, but somehow fires people with a desire to respond, to do something.

Gladwell's Mavens (derived from the Yiddish word for accumulating knowledge) also have a crucial role to play in creating social epidemics, but they are different to connectors. Mavens not only accumulate knowledge, they seem somehow to know which buttons to press in making that knowledge useful in a particular context – and then they want to share that knowledge. "The critical thing about Mavens, though, is that they aren't passive collectors of information... What sets them apart is that once they figure out how to get [the best] deal, they want to tell you about it too" (p 60).

Gladwell's Mavens are "information brokers, sharing and trading what they know" (p 69).

> For a social epidemic to start.. some people are actually going to have to be persuaded to do something.. Mavens are data banks. They provide the message. Connectors are social glue: they spread it. But there is a select group of people – Salesmen – with the skills to persuade us when we are unconvinced of what we are hearing, and they are as critical to the tipping of word of mouth epidemics as the other two groups (p 70).

Gladwell's third category is Salesmen. My children are all great salesmen. I see in them an ability I just don't have – the ability to 'close' a deal. Interestingly, Gladwell's thesis is very much linked to the non-verbal interactions that take place between people, often subconscious and barely perceivable. He doesn't discuss the ability of the outstanding seller to close deals on the phone. Or, in the case of St Paul, in a letter.

Of course, there is that danger again - of reading into Paul, the first century Jewish Christian, a modern set of characteristics which just don't fit. But that is always the hermeneutical problem, trying to be true to the original culture and context while seeking to discover how it might be relevant to the situations and struggles of our lives today.

SIMPLE IDEAS

I like simple and accessible ideas, such as the 'bolt on' idea I described in Chapter 9. Like Paul and his use of contemporary ideas about Lordship, I like to come up with ways of expressing things which surprise or undermine commonly held views or understandings. When we were living in the North East in the mid-1990s, I remember going to meet a senior executive of the region's voluntary sector. He described the work he was involved with and the extensive nature of the voluntary organisations and agencies he served. I asked him about his involvement with the Churches. He paused before responding. "I hadn't really ever thought of the Churches as being part of the voluntary sector".

That set me thinking. And shortly afterwards, I came up with this slogan: "The Churches – and faith communities – are the largest, best organised and most well resourced parts of the voluntary and community sector, only they don't realise it – so nor does anyone else". Part of the task of the social entrepreneur – Paul understood this well – is about building the confidence of your networks to help them see, and realise, their own potential.

I have long been a fan of co-operatives and, as described in Chapter 3, was involved in setting up the Co-operative Enterprise Centre in Hartlepool, and the Cleveland Co-operative Agency, in 1982. My thinking was inspired by social entrepreneurs like Robert Owen, who founded a co-operative community in New Lanark in the early 19th century, and three 19th century Anglican clergy who founded the Christian Socialist Movement, FD Maurice, JM Ludlow and Charles Kingsley (who wrote *The Water Babies*).

Their thinking was better than their practise, it could be said. In the 1850s, they put their energy and their money into the formation of worker co-operatives of tailors, shoemakers and even piano manufacturers, which – just like my Co-operative Enterprise Centre – failed gloriously!

I have also long been fascinated by the contribution of the 19th century Quaker industrialists to the humanisation of industry (Joseph Rowntree, John Cadbury, Titus Salt and others) and have spoken of their approach to Afghan people interested in trying to model different ways of reforming society in Afghanistan.

But the co-ops which have most inspired me are the Mondragon co-operatives (see Chapter 3). Rooted in Catholic Social Thought, they exemplify in the world of work, education, healthcare and much more the simple model of the 'Body' so loved by Paul. Actually structuring a dynamic way in which all people can share in responsible, accountable management and delivery has not been the Church's greatest strength down the ages! Ponderous committees may have replaced autocratic management but the vibrancy of the Church is best demonstrated by the impact of committed people worshipping and working together.

PAUL THE SCROUNGER

But you can't do much without money. And another feature of a social entrepreneur is being a good scrounger. Paul chose to earn his living as a tent maker, partly so that he could claim never to be dependent on others. Actually, it gave him great freedom to be himself and do what he wanted. I know the feeling – not wanting to be tied down, frustrated by the dreary accountability systems imposed by Government and institutions, including the Church (though actually, the Church has given me more freedom than I could ever have had working for another organisation). Paul knew the importance of money and went to great lengths to raise money for the poor in Jerusalem.

Horsley and Silberman see the Jerusalem collection as

> .. a co-ordinated act of leitourgia that emphasized their character as a worldwide movement of prophetic action. Although the Greek word leitourgia – whose English form is 'liturgy' – is usually translated as religious or cultic activity, the term in antiquity referred to any political-economic service rendered for the common good by the citizens of a city, the subjects of a king, or the devotees of a god. It was an active demonstration of power. And in offering funds to help the communities of the saints in Judea survive without dependence on wealthy patrons or surrender to the normal economic networks of the empire, the collection for Jerusalem could be seen as a political act (p 186).

Borg and Crossan have an interesting take on this. They argue that the Jerusalem Church was still 'modelling' true Christian community, with all members sharing and holding their goods in common. The trouble was, they couldn't easily survive without help and support from other (mainly Gentile) Christian communities.

I know that problem. The work I am involved in with Afghan Action in Kabul has always aimed to become self sufficient and, until the economic downturn in 2008, we were progressing well. We budgeted to sell £100,000 worth of carpets in 2008 and were well on track, helped by our best ever sale, in the Temple Church in the Strand, when we did £11,000 of sales one warm July evening. Then the economic downturn hit us. Through the autumn and winter of 2008 we really began to struggle – as we tried to sustain 180 people working for us in Kabul. I refer to this in Chapter 8.

We refocused our efforts not on employing people but on training and educating them and, since early 2009, we have gradually built up our work again, diversifying into training people to make clothes and uniforms as well as carpets.

We have classified our budget heads as 'income generation' – through carpet or clothing sales - and 'welfare' – including the costs of training, education, healthcare and food. The struggle to raise funds continues, because we choose to train and educate as well as produce, and to provide wages which are above the average. We are also able to provide midday meals for all staff and trainees, thanks to the generosity of the Supreme Foundation, who have played a major role in our latest project, to make quilts for refugees living in harsh conditions in tent camps around Kabul – and, through this, to train young women in sewing and tailoring.

Paul took money seriously. He courted those who had in order to obtain the assistance needed by those who had not.

Borg and Crossan speculate that the quid pro quo of the hard-fought agreement at Jerusalem, in which the conservative Jewish Christians conceded to the liberals, was this: that Paul and the Gentile Christians should donate to support James' utopian model community, where all held everything in common. Paul refers to this in Galatians: "they asked only one thing, that we remember the poor, which I was actually eager to do" (Galatians 1, 10). He explains this in greater detail in Romans 15:

> I am on my way to Jerusalem on an errand to God's people there. For Macedonia and Achaia have resolved to raise a fund for the benefit of the poor among God's people at Jerusalem... For if the Jewish Christians shared their spiritual resources with the Gentiles, the Gentiles have a clear duty to contribute to their material needs.. (verses 25 – 27).

From different references in Paul's letters (Galatians 2, 1 Corinthians 16, 2 Corinthians 8 - 9, Romans 15) and in Acts chapters 11, 20 and 21, we glean how the money was raised and delivered. There were some serious issues of pride and face at stake. Acts 21 is fascinating reading. It describes James' Jerusalem community and their reception of Paul with his collection money. When they heard Paul's description of his work among the Gentiles, "they gave praise to God" (Acts 21, 20).

And then the conditions kick in. Paul is told he needs to prove to the Jewish Christian believers that "you are indeed a practising Jew and observe the Law" (verse 24).

Paul and his Gentile companions have come to Jerusalem with the donations of the faithful. Paul has bent over backwards to please the Jewish Christians in Jerusalem. Now he must bite his lip and go through the ritual of purification at the Temple.

It all ends in tears. Paul gets spotted by Jews antagonistic to him and his faith, who accuse him of taking Gentiles into the Temple's inner courts – which is strictly forbidden. There is a riot. Paul is being beaten up when the Roman military appear and arrest him. After this, he is in captivity and, in due course, is sent to Rome.

A LAST COMMENT ABOUT PAUL

A last comment about Paul the social entrepreneur – he thrived on danger and coped with uncertainty. He was never quite sure what tomorrow would bring – but was not perturbed by that.

That doesn't suit everyone – in fact, it doesn't suit most people and it certainly doesn't suit well established institutions like Government and Church. But to grow a Church fit for the future, engaging with a culture not so much hostile as disinterested, the characteristics needed are passion, energy, risk, danger, excitement, challenge, commitment. They are the characteristics of that impossible giant of world history, Paul the apostle. And we need more Pauls if our practising of Jesus is to bring about the transformation in Church and society for which we long.

BIBLIOGRAPHY

John Barclay, *The Anthropology and History of the Gift* (unpublished draft chapter for a forthcoming book).

Marcus Borg and John Dominic Crossan, *The First Paul – reclaiming the radical visionary behind the Church's conservative icon* (SPCK 2009).

John Dominic Crossan and Jonathan L Reed, *In search of Paul* (SPCK 2005).

Jerome Murphy-O'Connor, *Paul: His Story* (OUP 2004).

Neil Elliot *Liberating Paul. The justice of God and the politics of the apostle* (Maryknoll, New York 1994).

Malcolm Gladwell, *The Tipping Point* (Little, Brown and Company 2000).

Richard A Horsley and Neil Asher Silberman, *The Message and the Kingdom. How Jesus and Paul ignited a revolution and transformed the ancient world* (Fortress Press Minneapolis 2002).

Wayne Meeks, *The First Urban Christians: The Social World of the Apostle Paul* (Yale University Press, 1983).

Jerome Murphy-O'Connor, *Paul. A critical life* (OUP 1996).

Albert Schweitzer, *The Philosophy of Civilization* (first published in 1923).

Matthew Syed, *Bounce The Myth of Talent and the Power of Practise* (Fourth Estate, 2011).

Paul Skirrow and Peter Winn (unpublished work on St Matthew's Gospel).

Wilf Wilde, *Nowhere to lay our head. Client rulers, the empire of oil and the anarchy of Jesus* (Melruha 2011).

Tom Wright *What St Paul Really Said* (Lion Hudson 1997).

A FINAL WORD

My family has had a huge influence on me and I am immensely grateful to them for their love and patience. I don't think I have been the easiest person to live with – though imagine what it would have been like having St Paul as a husband and father! My wife Angela and children Jackie, Chris, Andrew and their families have all helped to shape me and my thinking, as have my parents and brother Dave and sister Kate and countless others.

Of course, that's true for all of us.

One of the privileges of priesthood is the opportunity to encounter people at significant points in their lives – initiation/baptism; marriage; death/funeral. I rarely know the person whose funeral I am taking apart from what I have been told by family and friends. Weaving together a story of someone's life – as a crucial part of commending them to God and committing them to a future about which we know little but hope much – always makes me think about how people live on, not least through the influence they have had over others, through the looks and mannerisms and patterns of speech of their children and relatives, through the memories others have of them, though their ideas, their experience, their work.

My hope is that I will be remembered not for what I might have achieved (not a lot) nor for what I could have been or done, but for my efforts, albeit feeble in the extreme, to 'practise Jesus' in ways which made the world a better place and somehow enriched the lives of at least some of those I encountered. Actually, that is probably the hope of many of us. And the good news – to give Paul the last word – is this: ".. hope does not disappoint us, because God has poured out his love into our hearts by the Holy Spirit, whom he has given us" (Romans 5, 5).